THE RUM DIARY

Bruce Robinson started his career in cinema as an actor. Some of the world's greatest directors ignored him so he got into writing and finally directing films himself. Perhaps best known for *Withnail & I*, he is currently preparing a new film based on his novel, *The Peculiar Memories of Thomas Penman*. For a dozen years he has been working on a history of the Whitechapel Murders, which he hopes to publish in 2013 to coincide with the centenary of the death of 'Jack the Ripper'.

D1341609

BRUCE ROBINSON

The Rum Diary

A Screenplay

BASED ON THE NOVEL BY
Hunter S. Thompson

WITH AN INTRODUCTION BY
Johnny Depp

VINTAGE BOOKS
London

Published by Vintage 2011

2 4 6 8 10 9 7 5 3 1

Text and photographs copyright © GK Films LLC 2011
Introduction copyright © Johnny Depp 2011

Bruce Robinson has asserted his right under the Copyright,
Designs and Patents Act 1988 to be identified as the author of this work

This screenplay is based on the novel, *The Rum Diary*, by Hunter S.
Thompson, copyright © 1998 by the Gonzo International Corp.

Vintage
Random House, 20 Vauxhall Bridge Road,
London SW1V 2SA

www.vintage-books.co.uk

Addresses for companies within The Random House Group Limited can be
found at: www.randomhouse.co.uk/offices.htm

The Random House Group Limited Reg. No. 954009

A CIP catalogue record for this book is available from the British Library

ISBN 9780099555698

The Random House Group Limited supports The Forest Stewardship
Council (FSC®), the leading international forest certification organisation.
Our books carrying the FSC label are printed on FSC® certified paper. FSC is
the only forest certification scheme endorsed by the leading environmental
organisations, including Greenpeace. Our paper procurement policy can be
found at www.randomhouse.co.uk/environment

Set in Country Book 11 pt
Typeset by Palimpsest Book Production Limited, Falkirk, Stirlingshire

Printed and bound by CPI Group (UK) Ltd, Croydon, CR0 4YY

For The Pied.

FOREWORD

The year was 1997. Pre-production on the film version of the HST classic *Fear And Loathing In Las Vegas* was at full gallop. Having had the opportunity to know Hunter for a few years prior, he most generously welcomed me into his home and his life. Access all areas. We were good friends, but I had a job to do. I was there to sponge, to steal, thieve and/or pilfer as much of his soul as I could, and although, at times, it made him somewhat uncomfortable, he understood what I needed to do. He continued to give, and I continued to take. I was with him for months, day and night, night and day. I lived with him. Simply staying with Hunter was never an option. You had to *live*. And fortunately, since I loved the bastard so much, it suited me just fine. There was a mutual trust that ran deep. I even let the fucker shave my head.

One very late night, or perhaps, a very early morning (one never quite knew or cared for time when hunkered down in his fortified compound) we were rifling through all manner of treasures in what he would charmingly refer to as 'The War Room' (which was right across the hallway from my bedroom, where unbeknownst to me and my highly utilized ashtray, a full keg of gunpowder masqueraded as my bedside table), when I came across another old cardboard box, billowing with scruffy looking documents, submerged beneath a seemingly infinite sum of papers, books and general paraphernalia garnered from a life spent flirting precariously with the abyss.

The battered typescript was bound together by rubber bands, loosely housed amongst various worn and fatigued folders. On the cover of one, in Hunter's own hand, was scribbled *The Rum Diary*, the title of his unpublished novel from 1959. He wrote the book in his early twenties. And then stuffed it away. For all these years, the manuscript lay sequestered in a humble cardboard box, in the depths of Owl Farm. I was aware of the novel's existence, but thought it destined to sleep forever, along with other misplaced Hunter titles, most notably; *Prince Jellyfish* and *Polo Is My Life*. I was intrigued. We began to thumb through it, there and then, on the floor of 'The War Room', exchanging stacks of manuscripts, reading it to one another.

The Rum Diary was simply too good to remain lost.

As we read on, Hunter's enthusiasm got the better of both of us, and we were now officially riled up. Soon enough, such trusted friends and colleagues as Douglas Brinkley, the literary executor of HST's estate, and Warren Zevon, joined us in revisiting the juvenescent mayhem of those pages.

The novel was finally released in 1998 to rapturous acclaim, some forty years after it was originally conceived. Almost immediately, the subject of a film was broached, which was Hunter's idea. 'Hot damn . . . yessir, let's you and I produce this fucking caper together, Colonel! We'll have Hollywood groveling at our feet! They will crawl over a road of bones to get to us. Yessir! Fuck them! We need to have some fun!' And we did. Though Hunter's ardent prediction did not come to fruition quite as easily as we had hoped. Fiery hoops of all dimensions, covert bear-traps, woefully obstinate billfolds which neither Hunter or I, were remotely experienced in battling; such grueling corporate foreplay was certainly not our forte. But, as we had always practiced, together and individually, we were going to do this on our own terms. We set up a bar, the Tiki Hut, at my L.A. abode and held meetings well into the night. Many nights. Many meetings. We had no director attached, we had no screenwriter either, but we fought on, feverishly trying to get the ball rolling, while at every turn, found ourselves hindered by endless red tape, all manner of nefarious legal bindings, and

still no money; in short, we were taking a
fucking pounding. And then of course, there was
Hunter's temper, which occasionally manifested
itself thusly:

*Dear Holly, Okay, you lazy bitch, I'm getting
tired of this waterhead fuckaround that
you're doing with The Rum Diary. We are not
even spinning our wheels aggresivly. It's
like the whole Project got turned over to
Zombies who live in cardboard boxes under
the Hollywood Freeway . . .I seem to be
the only person who's doing anything about
getting this movie Made. What the hell do
you think Making a Movie is all about? Nobody
needs to hear any more of that Gibberish
about yr. New Mercedes & yr. Ski Trips &
how Hopelessly Broke the Shooting Gallery
is . . . If you're that fucking Poor you
should get out of the Movie Business. It
is no place for Amateurs & Dilletants who
don't want to do anything but "take lunch"
& Waste serious people's Time. Fuck this.
All you are is a goddamn Bystander, making
stupid suggestions & jabbering now & then
like some half-bright Kid with No Money
& No Energy & no focus except on yr. own
tits . . . I'm sick of hearing about Cuba
& Japs & yr. Yo-yo partners who want to
change the story because the violence makes
them Queasy. Shit on them. I'd much rather*

deal with a _Live_ asshole than a Dead worm
with No Light in his Eyes . . . If you
people don't _want_ to Do Anything with this
movie, just cough up the Option & I'll
talk to someone else. The only thing You're
going to get by quitting and curling up in
a Fetal position is relentless Grief and
Embarrassment. And the one thing you _won't_
have is Fun . . . Okay, That's my Outburst
for today. Let's hope that it gets Somebody
off the dime. And if you don't _Do Something_
QUICK you're going to Destroy a very good
idea. I'm in the mood to chop yr. fucking
hands off. R.S.V.P. HUNTER.

Needless to say, that episode didn't work out
too well, and our project lay dormant for some
time. But we weren't giving up.

There was one writer/director that we were
mutually obsessed with. I had known Bruce
Robinson casually for a number of years,
having a spent a few evenings with him, hunched
determinedly over various bars from Los Angeles
to London, whilst Hunter was well aware of his
masterpiece, _Withnail & I_. He was our Holy
Grail. Only one problem, I told Hunter. '_You do
remember that we had approached him with_ Fear &
Loathing . . . _But he'd already left the ugly
business of filmmaking behind, so it might take
some coaxing to reel him back in_'.

And some coaxing it did take, but we got Bruce in
2005. I was ecstatic. We had our man. However,
I was no longer in a position to deliver the
great news to my beloved brother of the dark
and bloody ground, who would have fully shared
in my joy. As we all know, Hunter had made
his remarkably abrupt exit from our tumultuous
sphere earlier that year. I had lost my dear
friend and co-conspirator. Sure as fuck wasn't
going to give up now.

Bruce proceeded to take the book, expertly
morphing Hunter's work into one of the finest,
funniest screenplays that I've ever had the honor
to be associated with. He was effortlessly able
to tap into Hunter's mind, tap into Hunter's
sense of anarchy, harness that distinct Thompson
vernacular, preserving the never more pertinent
themes of the book in this ever more capitalist,
homogenized world. I know Hunter would be proud
of what Bruce managed to achieve, both on the
page and on the screen. He perfectly retained
that humor, that magic, and most of all, that
vital, ebullient, HST spirit.

And it was that very spirit to which we paid
our daily respects to each morning. Our ritual
consisted of Chivas Regal, one generous dose
of; a highball glass filled to the brim with
ice and placed upon the arm of HST's designated
director's chair, complete with script and

smokes, into which forefingers would be immersed, and the clinging whiskey dabbed behind the ears as a token of good luck which succeeded in guiding us triumphantly throughout the shoot.

It would be impossible for me to try and encapsulate my love for this work, or its authors, by the poor use of some mawkish, cack-handed phrase. Instead, I'll simply state that there is something beautiful, something forlorn, something dangerous, something fiercely veracious about *The Rum Diary*; a tale of misspent youth, searching for a voice amid the sun and free-flowing rum of late '50's Puerto Rico that everyone should taste.

I did and am proud to have partaken, if not only for the experience of finally realizing the dream of working with the genius that is Bruce Robinson, our new brother in the struggle, but also for the road travelled with The Good Doctor, and to have played some part in bringing a lost sliver of his formative existence back to life.

Hunter, we fucking did it.

Johnny Depp
London, August 2011

The RUM DIARY

A Screenplay

1 EXT. HORIZON. DAY.

*It is the year of our lord, nineteen
hundred and sixty and the airways
are soiled with a hit called
'Volare'. Music to heave along with.
Mr DEAN MARTIN at the mike.*

*In vigorous contrast we've got the
view. Nothing phony about this. Pink
coral in reefs of clear water under
a seriously blue sky. It could be a
postcard from heaven.*

Volare oh oh

*Right out there in the cloudless
void a red speck comes into picture.
It's a small biplane towing some
kind of banner. But it's way too
far off to identify.*

Cantare oh oh oh oh

*Suddenly the candy-coloured plane
skipping paradise is all the picture
there is. It punches into frame
close enough to smell the exhaust. I*

*don't know how it happened, but
somehow the plane and song get into
an audio-visual sync, our hearts
borne aloft in aeronautical joy.*

2   INT. P.O.V. PILOT. AIRPLANE. DAY.

*Sunlight flares into the cockpit as
the pilot turns it around. He's
flying at about two hundred feet and
DEAN is on the breeze. Sparkling
ocean becomes stone-white sand, and
beyond is the big island. You can
see people on the beaches and now
their hotels. Tower after tower
compete for space on the shore, like
one side of a zip.*

3   EXT. P.O.V. FROM SOMEWHERE IN THE
     BAY. DAY.

*It's already clear what the plane is
up to. Hauling thirty yards of
advertising it works the hotels,
tiresome as a fly. See it once and
you get the message but the happy
sunbathers are required to see it
again and again. You can read it
from the beaches but not from here,
and no one's looking anyway, not
even the CAMERA. Isolating a*

*concrete monstrosity it moves in
towards an upper floor.*

4   INT. BEDROOM/BALCONY. HIGHRISE
    HOTEL. DAY.

*A room behind one of the balconies.
Night clings on and curtains are
still drawn. Outside something
passes with the discretion of a
freight train. A man on a bed
moans, one eye exploring the rudi-
ments of vision. It looks like a
bullet hole. The misuse of alcohol
can't be ruled out.*

*There's chaos on the floor. Clothes
and books spill from a suitcase, plus
compromised food remains, bent coat
hangers and a portable typewriter.*

*Weaving a passage through, feet
negotiate more paperbacks, scattered
newspapers, ashtrays and empty
bottles. The drone of an approaching
airplane intensifies as the feet
arrive at lime-green drapes. A
curtain is drawn aside and beyond
are the realities of daylight. A
face looks out, reacting unfavourably.
About thirty-five years old with an*

*animal of a hangover. It seems his
equilibrium took the brunt, and as
he steps onto the balcony he must
seek stability in the rail. Tropical
vistas at either side and vertigo
fifteen floors down. A SHOCKINGLY
RED PLANE becomes parallel with his
vision. It tows its message up the
beach: 'Puerto Rico welcomes Union
Carbide'.*

5   INT. BATHROOM/BEDROOM. HOTEL. DAY.

*A mouth guzzles direct from a tap,
and now a face stares back from the
mirror. Handsome despite the
carnage, and nothing aspirin can't
handle. But never mind that. His
face is plastered in some kind of
evil grease that he determines is
lipstick. But from whence did it
come? Was there a women in here? Is
she still in the fucking bed? Relief
she isn't is simultaneous with a
ringing doorbell.*

                    KEMP
      Who is it?

*It's room service and it says so.
KEMP gets it focused.*

KEMP
. . . Leave it out there,
I'll get to it . . .

*But the voice wants a signature. The
door gets opened on a security
chain, and KEMP looks suspiciously
at a WAITER.*

What is it? Is it eggs?

WAITER
. . . I don't know, sir, I
didn't order it . . .

*Whatever it is comes in on a
trolley. The WAITER sets up places
for two orders and KEMP swallows
multiple aspirins.*

WAITER
You want some water with that?

KEMP
Not right now . . .

WAITER
Looks like you had a night?

*Is that what it looks like? KEMP
fights off an aspirin gag.*

> WAITER
>
> Is someone joining you? I got
> two breakfasts here.

> KEMP
>
> That's OK. She left, I'll eat
> them both . . .

*He Zippos a cigarette [Menthol
Kool], and whips the lid off eggs.
'They look perfect'. But the WAITER
is looking at something else. A
small refrigerator [mini bar] is
part of the debris. Someone hauled
it out and tried to rifle it open.
No luck with coat hangers and kicked
shit out of it. KEMP is aware of
the WAITER's interest.*

> KEMP
> *(re. fridge)*
>
> I intended to bring that to the
> attention of a member of a staff
> . . . I had some difficulty
> getting it to open . . .

> WAITER
>
> It's the little key, on the
> door key . . .

                    KEMP
    Oh, right . . .
         (finds it)
    I was looking for some nuts.

The mini bar is on its back. On knees KEMP successfully opens it, revealing a trove of miniature liquor bottles.

    I tend to avoid alcohol . . .
         (looking up)
    When I can . . .

Maybe time for a smile but there's a slam cut into titles. HOUND DOG TAYLOR & THE HOUSE ROCKERS hit it loud with inimitable blues. This song is called 'The Sun Is Shining'.

6   INT/EXT. TAXI/BOULEVARD. SAN JUAN. DAY.

Slam right into the mouth of fat chrome. It's the radiator grill of a '53 de Soto. And indeed the sun is shining. Flamboyant trees make it a pretty street. But the houses that once looked out onto the beach now look out onto hotels.

I don't like describing camera moves.
But this is tracking back in front
of the cab until a cut takes us
inside. There's a DRIVER who looks
like he needs sleep and a man in the
back behind a newspaper entitled The
Daily Star.

                    DRIVER
        Primera vez en San Juan?

                    KEMP
        I don't speak Spanish.

So that's the end of that relation-
ship. There's a sharp change in
KEMP'S appearance. Everything that
needed it got attention. He's
showered and shaved and behind Ray
Bans. Shakes out a Kool and a Zippo
momentarily flares.

By now they're speeding along a
causeway. A radiant sea with occa-
sional fisherman doing their thing.
All in all the day's shaping nicely,
and with a pocketful of miniatures
it might get even better. He swal-
lows one and considers another.
Outside the landscape is changing
into suburbs of San Juan. The taxi

*is moving but wouldn't be anywhere
else. This is dog eat dog and screw
the lights.*

7   INT/EXT. TAXI/STREETS. OLD SAN
JUAN. DAY.

*This part of town is picturesquely
colonial [what guidebooks describe
as a Spanish Flavour]. You can
barely see for car exhaust but the
DRIVER finally thinks he's there.*

                    KEMP
    El Star? San Juan Star?

*Shit-English and indifferent, the
DRIVER nods at a street.*

    What's the matter with going
    down it?

                    DRIVER
    Quatro cinco . . . No change.

*KEMP has already slammed the door.
Abandoned and miffed at the rip-off,
he pays the bastard and heads down a
hill.*

8   EXT. CALLE PLACE COLON. SAN JUAN. DAY.

So many motor horns in the city it takes a while to understand why they're concentrated here. Traffic is blocked in a honking cacophony and cops try to clear it. Various drivers have lost their rag and shout about it in Spanish.

For reasons yet unknown a contingent of angry workmen are protesting in the street. If they've got a placard they wave it. If they've got a bugle they blow it. Some have rotten fruit and look for targets. Clearly something has made them very cross with the offices of THE DAILY STAR.

KEMP heads towards it but isn't associated with the building until he reaches its steps.

Suddenly he's converted into some kind of 'black leg' [whatever that might be in Spanish]. Doors are locked and he hits a bell. Nothing happens until a cop arrives with a key. Grapefruits and mouldy lemons splatter glass doors as KEMP is allowed in.

9   INT. NEWS ROOM [SECOND FLOOR].
    DAILY STAR. DAY.

    It's a big room with all the usual
    paraphernalia of putting a newspaper
    together. Virtually every cliche is
    evident [typewriters, telex machines,
    and ceiling fans that can't cope].
    The air is almost blue with
    cancerous smoke.

    About a dozen desks in business, and
    most are on the telephone. At one a
    journalist hammers it into a type-
    writer. Got a phone clamped to his
    neck, typing it as he hears it.

                    KEMP
        I'm looking for Mr Lotterman?

                    DONAVON
        End of the room.

    He slams the carriage back, and
    KEMP weaves through desks. The big
    room terminates in offices. One with
    a very shut door is evidently the
    one KEMP was looking for. Focusing
    his act, he taps on frosted glass
    and gets a frosty reply.

> VOICE (O.S.)
Not now.

The rebuff was unexpected but explained by a passing voice.

> SALA
He's having a Friday Crisis.

The voice belongs to a man behind glasses. Cigar between teeth he carries Kodacrome boxes with a cup of coffee balanced on top. Of indifferent age he needs shampoo and is possibly in need of rehab. But despite the unlaundered aura there's something attractive about him. Dumping his boxes onto a nearby desk he smiles across at the stranger.

> SALA
You Kemp?
>   (affirmative)
He was expecting you yesterday?

> KEMP
We had some weather . . .

> SALA
Yeah, I heard.

A red light glows on a phone, he heads for a coffee maker.

. . . big snow in New York?
He's still on the call, you
want some coffee?

                    KEMP
          (negative)
What's all the fuss out in
front?

                    SALA
You came in the front? We
don't use that door. Not when
Los Jibaros pitch up.

                    KEMP
What do they want?

                    SALA
I dunno, some fucked idea of
a living wage, they been out
there on and off for months
          (offering hand)
By the way, my name is Sala,
Bob Sala, staff photographer.

> KEMP
> Pleased to meet you, Bob.

They already like each other. The phone light goes out.

> SALA
> He's off. You might wanna try another subservient knock?

KEMP heads for the hot door. Gets a last bit of advice.

> Don't notice the wig.

10 INT. LOTTERMAN'S OFFICE/NEWS ROOM. DAY.

The first thing you notice about LOTTERMAN is the wig [or rather toupee]. It's like a limp hat with an unfortunate colour scheme. Lifting a glance towards KEMP he gets back to some heavyweight reading. A red pencil is frequently used. Without interest in anything else he finds a voice.

> LOTTERMAN
> If you're who I think you are, you better sit down.

The instruction is followed and KEMP looks about. LOTTERMAN is something out of the old school, mid sixties, striped shirt and suspenders. One or two things about his office are worth pointing out. There's a big map of Puerto Rico on a wall and crossed flags of the same country and the USA on his desk.

Behind him are windows looking out into the street. The protesters are raising volume and there is a wail of distant sirens. More editing with the red pencil, and eyes twist back with a reference to KEMP's sunglasses.

>   LOTTERMAN
>   . . . you find it a little
>   bright in here?

>   KEMP
>   I'd take them off, but I have
>   a medical condition.

>   LOTTERMAN
>   What d'you mean, you're blind?

>   KEMP
>   Conjunctivitis, sir.

LOTTERMAN

The old, 'red eye'.

A slow fan swivels on his desk. He tosses the edit aside.

You arrive at a very trying time, Mr Kemp, one of those days stacking up. So if you don't mind, we'll skip the niceties and get right to it?

KEMP

It's how I like to proceed.

LOTTERMAN
(finds a file)
I was impressed by your C.V., you've worked your way up some interesting titles, and I like the 'fluent Spanish' . . .
The only thing that bothers me about it is the bits that are missing? What happened between St Louis & New York?

KEMP

A time I'm trying to forget.

LOTTERMAN
How well are you doing?

KEMP

Not so good.

LOTTERMAN

Then let's hear it?

KEMP

It was one of those 'star-crossed'
things . . . she was young, and
innocent, and I . . .

LOTTERMAN

I'm not looking for Edith
Wharton . . . just the gist?

KEMP

. . . a bad divorce, I lost
everything . . .

LOTTERMAN

And then?

KEMP

Then I taught English, basic-
ally the poets . . . I
forgot how many years, but my
passion was always to get
back to journalism.

                    LOTTERMAN
Why Puerto Rico?

                       KEMP
You know how it is, when
you're starting over? You weigh
up the jobs . . . some more
possible than others . . .

                    LOTTERMAN
I didn't think you were down
here to spite the *Washington
Post*. This C.V. is a bunch of
bullshit . . . you're either
overqualified or you're lying.

*The door flies open and in comes a
man who doesn't need to knock. He's
Spanish-American and that'll do for
now.*

                    SEGURRA
This is two days off the
wire.
            (proffering a telex)
A day dead. We don't have it.

*LOTTERMAN'S shallow sigh is a study
in minimalistic fury.*

LOTTERMAN
What's the matter with Moburg?
He's about as much use as a
dug-up body?

*A resigned and bitter smile takes
over. There may be an issue of
blood pressure. SEGURRA and his
telex are gone.*

The problem with this newspaper, Mr Kemp, is that I am
among many who don't enjoy
reading it. We have an ailing
circulation, and I only have
to look around this building
to understand why . . . a
lack of commitment, and too
much *self-indulgence* . . . I
got people on salary here who
come in like guests . . . on
days like this, I feel like
I'm running the thing on my
own . . . So, I'm looking
for some enthusiasm . . .
some energy . . . some *fresh
blood*, and the question I'm
asking myself is how much
alcohol is usual in yours?

KEMP

My fresh blood?

LOTTERMAN

How much do you drink?

KEMP
(*weighing a shrug*)
I suppose, at the upper end of
social. I'm poised to give up.

LOTTERMAN

Puerto Rico might not be the
best place on earth to do
that.

*Is KEMP jittery with nerves? Or
jittery with withdrawal?*

Don't look so anxious, Kemp,
I wouldn't be paying for a
hotel if I hadn't already
hired you . . . but this
isn't the last chance saloon,
and I got no place for
another heavy drinker which,
I perceive from the condition
of eyeballs behind sunglasses,
you might very well qualify
as?

Police sirens are close now. The vibe isn't comfortable.

                    KEMP
          This is a medical condition,
          Mr Lotterman. I know it might
          look like something else.

                  LOTTERMAN
          It looks like a fucking hang-
          over.

By now the SIRENS have arrived and LOTTERMAN is on his feet at the windows, staring down into the street. Satisfaction at the view is obvious, he beckons KEMP to share it.

[P.O.V.] Police in riot gear erupt from vans and assault everyone in the vicinity. Helmets, and trun- cheons, and kicking. One zealous moron repeatedly puts the boot in.

                  LOTTERMAN
          That's the kind of commitment
          I like to see in a man . . .
                    (*showing teeth*)
          . . . determination, balanced
          with appropriate humanity.

*He turns to KEMP with manic eyes,
their faces very close.*

Which side d'you dress, Kemp?

                    KEMP
I beg your pardon?

                LOTTERMAN
Politics?

                    KEMP
I kind of hang in the middle.

*While the fracas continues LOTTERMAN
discovers a cigar in the ashtray.
Accepts a light from KEMP who Zippos
a Kool.*

                LOTTERMAN
This is a schitzoid society . . .
          (exuding smoke)
They got two languages, two
flags, two anthems,
and two loyalties . . .
We bring them stuff they
never had, and they either
hate it or want more of
it . . .

Opening the door he escorts KEMP
back into the News Room.

. . . it's a reluctant part
of America, like an England
with tropical fruit. Hey,
Bob, you're the man I wanna
see.

SALA is where we left him. His boss
forces introductions.

This is Paul Kemp. He's
joining us from New York.

                    SALA
Yeah, we already met.

                 LOTTERMAN
          (*other faces*)
Mr Clive Donavon, Sports
. . . Mr Hubert, our
accountant . . .
          (*to SALA*)
Do me a favour, will you,
show him around a little
. . . the dos and don'ts
. . . introduce him to some
of the guys . . .

SALA

I'll take him up to Al's.

LOTTERMAN

The hell you will, take him
to the library, pull out some
volumes. I want him to get a
sense of the paper.
(steering KEMP)
Go back a few years, take
some notes, paying particular
attention to the bowling
alleys.
(navigating desks)
Bowling and bowling alleys is
big, they're up like mush-
rooms, a new one premieres
every week.

DONAVON

You been to Puerto Rico
before?

KEMP

No.

LOTTERMAN

You're gonna fall right into
it. There's a boom on, Kemp,
it's an open door . . . Play
it right, you can surf the

place. What do you know about
Horoscopes?

                    KEMP
Nothing.

                    LOTTERMAN
If I can write one, you can.

*They arrive at a desk [star charts,
astrological books], it's clear somebody was working this junk until
recently.*

It's every day with a special
'Star's Star' featured
Saturdays . . . Betty Grable
. . . Neil Sedaka . . . that
kind of thing . . .
          (selling it)
You'll find everything you
need right here . . . It's
called 'Madam La Zonga
Predicts'.

                    KEMP
What happened to Madam La
Zonga?

SALA
He got cancelled.

KEMP
What do you mean, fired?

LOTTERMAN
They raped him to death.

KEMP
They raped him to death?

SALA
There are very few places on
this island I'd decline to
visit, but the toilets
frequented by sailors on the
west side of Candado Pier is
one.

LOTTERMAN
La Zonga died in a cubical.
        (eyes asking)
Not artistic are you, Kemp?

KEMP
No, sir.

LOTTERMAN
You might wanna reconsider
those refrigerated cigarettes,

they don't do anything for
you.

11 INT. ARCHIVES AND LIBRARY. DAILY
STAR. DAY.

*Archives of the newspaper include
volume after volume of back issues.
There are several tables with
reading lamps and filing cabinets
one end. Extracting a file, SEGURRA
glances down the room at KEMP. He
sits with an overflowing ashtray and
stack of volumes. Another page turns
revealing another Schmuck with a cup
in some bowling alley.*

*KEMP raises eyes as a man in a
snazzy suit walks in. Like a TV
presenter, with instant charisma,
everything about him reeks confi-
dence. On his way to confer with
SEGURRA, he smiles at KEMP, apparently aware what he's doing here.*

*The last volume is replaced with the
next and KEMP lights another. Gets
an unexpected hand on his shoulder.
White teeth and cologne, the man in
the suit is already leaving.*

                    SANDERSON
I looked over your stuff.
          (gets a blank)
The cuttings you sent to
Lotterman? Good writing.

                    KEMP
Thanks.

                    SANDERSON
I won't disturb you now.
          (finds it)
We'll talk . . .

*He snaps a business card on the
desk like he just won at poker.
Before there's time to read it
SANDERSON is gone.*

12 INT. COMPOSITOR/PRINT ROOM. DAILY
STAR. DUSK.

*Like a subterranean parking lot full
of machines, even the air throbs in
here. Fresh newspapers pass overhead
and descend on a conveyor. It's as
good an opportunity as any for a
reveal. SALA all but hollers to get
heard.*

SALA

. . . they put in automated
packing machines about six
months ago . . . mechanised
almost everything.

*A river of newspapers heads for the
rear of the building. Here's where
they get packed and slung into
waiting vans.*

. . . there used to be fifty
guys down here, now there's
five . . hence happiness in
the street . .

*He expertly snatches a newspaper.
Slaps it over to KEMP.*

Souvenir. Day one.

*Twilight outside security gates.
Someone SALA recognises is on his
way through. It will slam itself
automatically.*

Hold the gate.

*Out they all go leaving the metal
door to get on with it.*

13 INT/EXT. AL's BAR/TERRACE. SAN
    JUAN. DUSK.

*A bar at one end and open terrace
at the other. Bamboo furniture and a
string of coloured lights.
It's a dive except it's upstairs and
for anyone who wants it there's a
view over the port. But no one's
looking and no one's listening to a
black guy sweating nostalgia from a
piano.*

*Meanwhile the place is half full of
staff from The Star [who'll get
introduced if they need to be]. SALA
and company have just arrived at the
bar where shots are already poured.
The man who held the gate, WOLSLEY,
is fighting middle age but losing
with the gut. He passes a grubby
menu to KEMP. A hamburger it has to
be. SALA raises his rum in a toast.*

                SALA
    Here's to pretty women with
    filthy thoughts.

*WOLSLEY is a seedy-looking cove,
almost certainly English.*

WOLSLEY
How was the induction?

KEMP
Somewhat fraught.

SALA
No disrespect, Paul, but he
didn't have a lot of choice.
        (swallows rum)
You know how many people
applied for the job? One.
You.

KEMP
        (amused)
Is that right? Even then I
thought I'd blown it, he
zeroed in on my weakest spot.

WOLSLEY
Which is what?

KEMP
Two and a half unpublished
novels, and references of
equal fiction.

WOLSLEY
You're a novelist?

KEMP

In a manner of speaking, I
can't even get it read . . .
so I figured I'd do some
words for money, see how it's
looking in a year or two.

SALA

At *El Star*?
    (flags more rum)
I hate to tell you this
on the way in, but this
publication is on the way
out . . . and as far as
I'm concerned, it can't
come soon enough.

WOLSLEY

Not gonna happen.

SALA

You like a little vonga on
that? I'll give you 13 to
2 this thing's over by
June, they're gonna cut the
cord.

KEMP

Then why put in new
machinery?

WOLSLEY
Precisely my point, and he
can't answer it.

SALA
Like I'm tired of arguing the
obvious? C'mon, let's eat.

WOLSLEY
I gotta see a man about a
horse. Good to meet you, Paul.

*He becomes gone and SALA finds a
table. 'These Foolish Things' on the
piano and lights coming on all over
town.*

SALA
Another night unfolds over
old San Juan . . .

KEMP
You been here long?

SALA
Too long, this place is like
someone you fucked and they're
still under you.

KEMP
Then why don't you quit?

(lights it)
Life's full of exits.

                    SALA
Because I'm waiting for it to
collapse, so I get the
pay-off. Three grand redundancy
puts me in Mexico . . .
          (looking)
Don't . . . look . . . left . . .

*Something unpleasant passes and
loiters in the vicinity.*

That's an introduction you
don't wanna have.

                    KEMP
Who is he?

                    SALA
A living example of the state
this paper's in . . . His
name's Moburg, our crime and
religious affairs corres-
pondent. Lotterman can't fire
him because he never sees
him, he's rarely out in
daylight.

                    KEMP
Looks like he enjoys a drink?

                    SALA
The entire sub-structure of
his brain is eaten away with
rum. Bits and pieces work
depending on the time of day.

                    KEMP
That is not a wholesome look.

*When you see MOBURG you'll know
what he's talking about.*

                    SALA
You wouldn't want to get in
the way of his breath. I'm
telling you, this enterprise
is doomed . . . there's maybe
three or four professionals
in the building: Donavon,
Wolsley, Frankie Morrel and
me, running the entire show.

                    KEMP
Who's Hal Sanderson?

*It's a gold-edge business card and
KEMP hands it across.*

In the library? Who is he?

                    SALA
He used to work for the
paper, now he's what he says
he is, a P.R. consultant,
selling this place street by
street to the Yanquis . . .
        (drinks)
. . . he keeps a greasy
little bastard of a contact
called Segurra . . .

                    KEMP
I saw him . . . we didn't
meet . . .

                    SALA
I wouldn't bother, piss on the
make . . . the boy Segurra is
into property wickedness . . .
I'm not sure where Sanderson
fits . . .
        (returns card)
. . . neither are to be
trusted, but Sanderson's worth
cultivation, got some good
connections, good for some
freelance.
        (a change of song)
Anything but 'Night and

Fucking Day'. This place is depressing me beyond belief tonight . . . You're at Plage Xanadu, right?
> (correct)

C'mon, I'll give you a ride.

KEMP

What about the hamburgers?

SALA

We'll take another snifter, and eat them in the street.

14 EXT. STREET. OLD SAN JUAN. NIGHT.

It's a hot Caribbean night, music here and there and moonlight everywhere. Gas-lamps on a steep cobblestone hill. As they descend SALA and KEMP munch hamburgers, the latter a tad unsteady on his feet, but more likely fatigue than booze. Twisting in the street, he stares up at breathtaking stars.

KEMP
> (quoting Keats)

'Bright star, would that I were steadfast as thou art' . . .

. . . I never seen so many
stars, how would I write them
down . . .

                    SALA
. . you don't have to take
it too literally . . the dead
guy got it from books . .

                    KEMP
I didn't exactly mean that . . .
          (chuckling)
. . . all I want is to be a
writer, and I am a Madam La
Zonga . . .

*SALA gets the irony but doesn't
find it as funny as KEMP.*

                    SALA
Are you kaput?
          (negative)
. . . then I got the perfect
hellhole for our nightcap.

                    KEMP
Not tonight . . . tonight is
swimming night . . . they got
a pool with a palm tree, I
been thinking about it all day.

SALA
Dog Shit! Dog fucking shit!

He squeezes his hamburger into a ball of as yet unexplained rage, and pitches it like a grenade into a nearby wall.

Look what they did to my car.

The car is a tiny open-roofed Fiat 500 and some moron has filled it with garbage. Obviously a revenge attack. Rotten vegetables and fish parts erupt out over the sidewalk.

KEMP
Who did it?

SALA
Union goons and other allied bastards.

With eyes aflame he launches a cantaloupe into the darkness.

15 EXT. BOULEVARD. OLD SAN JUAN. NIGHT.

Garbage falls down the highway like confetti. Empty cans and other unpleasantries spin away.

*Craning away from the road the
CAMERA tracks fast behind the
little car. Almost all the rubbish
is gone and the ejections become
sporadic.*

> SALA (O.S.)
> These guys don't know which
> side it's buttered . . .
> They want an enemy? They got
> me.

16 INT. FIAT 500 CONVERTIBLE/
BOULEVARD. NIGHT.

*This is one of history's smallest
cars. Space is further reduced
by the presence of a large domestic
wireless set. Wires dangle but
the dial glows and apparently it
works.*

> SALA
> . . . this is what you get
> for sympathising . . .

*He tosses out a pineapple tuft,
KEMP produces miniatures.*

> KEMP
> You want a drink?

SALA

Where'd you get them?

KEMP

They put them in the room. I got Cointreau, Tia Maria and gin.

SALA

I'll take a gin.
        (swigs)
How long's he putting you up?

KEMP

Didn't say anything about it.

SALA

He will.
        (smelling it)
There's something lingeringly putrescent . . . ?

KEMP

        (finding it)
Oh my God.

SALA

Throw it out.

A sizable and stinking lobster vanishes into the night.

17 EXT. FORECOURT. LA PLAGE XANADU
   HOTEL. NIGHT.

*Money making an eye-sore of itself
for twenty floors. There are
circumcised palms and glamorous
autos, plus a black DOORMAN in a
brown top hat. The Fiat rattles in
looking like a car that won't get
its door opened and it doesn't.*

> SALA
>
> I was thinking, if you need
> somewhere, I got a room for
> rent . . . not the best
> address in town, but it's got
> a fridge and TV, sixty a
> month . . .

> KEMP
>
> Sounds inviting.
> *(sprucing up)*
> I might remention that.

*He's out and heading for the HAT.
SALA calls after him.*

> SALA
>
> Meanwhile, bleed it.

18 INT. FOYER/SWIMMING POOL. XANADU
HOTEL. NIGHT.

*Inside looks like outside except it's
populated by Yanquis, not a few of
whom wear party togs. Anyone who
passes KEMP will be aware of his
association with garbage. He arrives
at glass doors with an illuminated
swimming pool beyond. A COMBO in white
dinner jackets puts out the sound and
some kind of ritzy party is in
progress. You need an invite to join
the fun and KEMP doesn't have one.
His entrance is blocked by a fussy
looking little anus of a MAITRE D.*

                    KEMP
        I was hoping for a swim?

                    MAITRE D
        The pool's closed tonight . . .

*Meanwhile he's only too delighted to
usher in the invited. Guests in the
vicinity are aware of the intrusive
STENCH.*

                    KEMP
        What's going on here?

>   MAITRE D
>   The Union Carbide party . . .
>   It's a private function . . .

*Not a few of the elderly ladies
sport face-lifts of the wind-tunnel
variety. One such is presently
looking at KEMP with an expression
of distaste.*

*She's permanently doing about a
hundred miles an hour. As KEMP
pushes off he leans confidingly into
the ear of her ancient husband.*

>   KEMP
>   She's spending too much time
>   on the motorcycle . . .

19 EXT. PRIVATE BEACH. XANADU HOTEL.
NIGHT.

*Bright red paint reveals itself as
a paddle-boat. Shoes on laces
around his neck, KEMP pushes into
the moonlight. It seems the
booze has finally registered and
slumping back he peddles an
erratic course towards a horizon of
stars.*

*Fifty yards from the shore and
nothing but lapping water, although
if you bother you can just about
hear the music.*

*Too wasted to swim he snaps a
Cointreau and for a moment thinks
he's hallucinating. A VISION has
arisen from the deep. Honey-blonde
hair drenches her shoulders and eyes
blue as bluebells. At a glance she
looks entirely naked and is possibly
the most beautiful girl he has ever
seen.*

> GIRL
> I'm sorry, I didn't realise
> anyone was there . . . I
> thought it was just floating.

> KEMP
> It is just floating.

> GIRL
> Are you doing what I'm doing?

> KEMP
> I don't think so . . .
> *(sitting up)*
> What are you doing?

                    GIRL
Escaping a dreadful party, I
just snuck out and unzipped.

                    KEMP
That's very courageous of you.

*Translucent water like she's dancing
naked in moonlight.*

I thought maybe you were a
mermaid . . . they tell me
the coast's infested with
them.

                    GIRL
I'm from Connecticut . . . my
boyfriend's making a speech.
          (killer smile)
It takes exactly twenty-one minutes.

                    KEMP
So it's pointless me inviting
you for a drink?

                    GIRL
What you got?

                    KEMP
I mean, at the bar?

GIRL
Yeah, pointless. I gotta go
before they wonder where I
went.

KEMP
Wait a minute, what's your
name?

GIRL
Let's keep it a secret.

KEMP
I don't even know it?

GIRL
. . . Then you'll keep it
even better . . . sweet to
meet you . . .

*He stares after her naked ass, drunk
and utterly smitten.*

KEMP
All right, your star-sign?
I'm an experienced astronomer.

GIRL
You could try Pisces, the
fish.

*She disappears into reflections of
the hotel and is gone.*

> KEMP
> Oh God, why did she have to
> happen? Just when I thought I
> was doing good without her?

*He swigs and slumps back in the
seat, eyes investigating the
heavens. How anybody can make
sense of that mess is beyond him,
but what of the girl under the
sign of Pisces?*

> . . . I don't know if I
> want to live in Connecticut
> anyway . . .

20 INT. BOWLING ALLEY. SAN JUAN. DAY.

*KEMP is hunched in the bowling
alley like he's been watching the
same ball travel a thousand miles.
P.O.V. of the ball as it careens
down the alley. Pins disintegrate
and the machine resets them and a
CHAMPION with a mountainous gut
punches the air in joy. From time
to time flashbulbs pop. But here
comes another ball and the same*

*thing happens over again. This
is the dictionary definition
of the word repetition. Hell
probably looks something like
this.*

> KEMP
> *(taking notes)*
> what would you say you like
> most about Puerto Rico?

> CHAMP
> The alleys and the casinos.
> *(his WIFE)*
> She likes the Duty Free.

*Both are dressed like four year
olds, shorts and ankle socks.*

> WIFE
> . . . the more you spend,
> the more you save . . .

*Dialogue continues over a baleful
montage. Fat hands work slot
machines, faces in glee as they win.
Nothing is more significant in their
day than the appearance of THREE
RED CHERRIES.*

> KEMP (O.S.)
> Have you seen a lot of the island?

> CHAMP (O.S.)
> We never leave the hotel.

> WIFE (O.S.)
> It isn't safe.

> KEMP
> But you're having fun?

> CHAMP
> Oh yeah, a lotta fun.

And back into the nightmare as another ball thunders down the endless alley and fresh skittles shatter. KEMP wears a new white Panama that he tilts over his eyes. Seeks consolation in a miniature, overwhelmed by the crashing ten pins.

> KEMP (V.O.)
> Have some fun with a fucking Luger . . . these alleys are magnets to the glutton . . . they come off the boats like locusts . . . beasts of

obesity, asses that wouldn't
feel an arrow . . . the
Great Whites, probably the
most dangerous creatures on
earth . . .

*Is this another hallucination, or a
facet of fantasy realised? The
ten-pin replacing apparatus has just
put down a clutch of pristine
bottles. Rum flagons stand in
waiting and here comes the ball. A
galaxy of booze and glass explode in
slow motion as the ball delivers a
perfect strike.*

21 INT. SALA'S DARKROOM. THE DAILY
STAR. DAY.

*A dissolve is already in progress.
At its end is violet light and a
developing picture of the CHAMP and
his WIFE.*

> SALA
There's your baby.
> (photo)
Walt and his Woman.

*He pulls it dripping from the tray
and hangs it on a line. KEMP is
perched somewhere on a stool in
dense cigar smoke.*

> KEMP
> Bowing alleys isn't what I
> had in mind.

> SALA
> Tread it till the snow melts,
> then join the exodus.

*There's a knock on the door and
SALA shouts, 'Red Light'. A voice
responds, 'Looking for Kemp?' and
it's LOTTERMAN.*

22 INT. NEWS ROOM. THE DAILY STAR. DAY.

*All the usual sounds and mess of
the News Room. LOTTERMAN and KEMP
walk through, the latter hearing
criticism.*

> LOTTERMAN
> *(re. manuscript)*
> . . . too many adjectives,
> too much cynicism . . .
> nobody wants what's wrong with
> the place, they want to read

what's right.

                    KEMP
It's a rewrite . . .

                 LOTTERMAN
I'm aware of that, and you
might want to rewrite the
title? Call it '10 Things I
Love about Puerto Rico'.

They've arrived at KEMP's desk.
LOTTERMAN makes a smile.

                 LOTTERMAN
How's the sobriety coming
along?

                    KEMP
I'm cutting down.

                 LOTTERMAN
By that I assume you mean the
size of the bottles?
          (hotel bill)
How does anyone drink one
hundred and sixty-one miniatures? You're averaging ninety-
three miniatures a week, they
must be stocking the thing
four times a day?

KEMP

They're not complimentary?

LOTTERMAN

No, Mr Kemp, they are not . . .
and neither is wine or long-
distance phone calls. As of
Monday, you are no longer a
resident at the Xanadu . . .

*The end of a sentence becomes the
beginning of a new one.*

. . . and what exactly brings
you into the building?

MOBURG

Don't hassle me, I got the X-
rays. I got less that a week
to live.

LOTTERMAN

'Hazle' you? What are you
talking about, you Swedish
Twerp?
    (instant anger)
It may have crossed what's
left of your mind that I'm
here to run a newspaper. We
got something called 'news'
going on out there, and as

far as you're concerned, I
may as well look out the
fucking window.
        (confronting him)
What d'you want in here? This
is a *newspaper*, there's
nothing for you in here.

MOBURG
Two of the best scoops you
ever had came outta my
brain, and you better moderate
you language or I'll go elsewhere.

LOTTERMAN
You'll go elsewhere? Elsewhere
where? You couldn't get work
as a fly repellant . . .

*MOBURG's face looks like someone
taking a difficult shit.*

. . . you're worthless,
Moburg, the last onion in the
jar . . .

MOBURG
Don't push me, Lotterman, I'm
dangerous when pushed . . .

                    LOTTERMAN
I know why you're here, you're
here because it's pay-day,
except in your case deferred
on a permanent basis. You're
fired.

                    MOBURG
You can't fire me, you owe
me money, and you better
pay it, or I'll come through
the roof and turn this
place into an insurance
claim.

                    LOTTERMAN
Are you threatening me?

                    DONAVON
Let's take it easy, guys?

                    MOBURG
You wanna suffer some Voodoo?

                    LOTTERMAN
You *twerp*.

*Grabbing the toupee MOBURG raises it
like a saucepan lid.*

> MOBURG
Eat the death pill, Lotterman.

A flashbulb explodes, catching the wig hovering at two feet.

> KEMP
C'mon, we're walking . . .

Rigid with indignation, but also attempting to reinstate dignity in respect of the toupee, LOTTERMAN allows himself to be led. KEMP fixes a destination on his office.

> LOTTERMAN
You hear what he said to me? This guy's my blood-pressure, this guy will kill me (and I want the negative of that picture destroyed).

He shouts at SALA [who took it]. KEMP keeps him walking.

I never want to see that animal in the building again . . . he is hygienically unacceptable . . . you see the side of his nose,

blackheads like Braille, they
should have him put down.

*They've arrived in the office before
KEMP realises the wig is on back to
front. But otherwise LOTTERMAN finds
focus.*

Moburg is history, outta here
at the earliest opportunity,
and the earliest opportunity
is you . . . You understand
what I'm saying, Kemp?

                KEMP
I think I get the drift.

              LOTTERMAN
I want you to immerse yourself in this paper, you got
the talent and I think you
got the will. Make it grow,
and you grow along with it.

*His enthusiasm seems genuine despite
the reversed hairdo.*

                KEMP
I'm not best placed to do
that.

LOTTERMAN
It's not my intention to keep
you on horoscopes, rewrites
and bowling alleys . . .
                (pulling $ wad)
. . . as a matter of fact, I'm
gonna move you now. Get a cab,
go out to the airport. The
Mayor of Miami's coming in,
make him sound nice. I want a
picture and an interview . . .
Make it work, Paul . . .

23 INT. TERMINAL. SAN JUAN AIRPORT. DAY.

*Open plan in the days before para-
noia hit. Several D.C.7. are parked
out in the heat. A coterie of
slick-suited Hispanics mill at the
windows waiting for the same flight
as KEMP. He props the bar with a
beer and battered suitcase, and like
the men with the suits has been
waiting for some time.*

SANDERSON (O.S.)
        (re. suitcase)
Are you leaving us already?

*Where did he arrive from? KEMP
looks pleasantly surprised.*

KEMP
I'm moving home, if this
mayor guy ever turns up
          (re. board)
. . . they keep changing
delayed to delayed . . .

SANDERSON rations a smile. Both
shift eyes to the SUITS.

Who are these guys?

          SANDERSON
Footnotes in the wake of a
deal. No one gives a fuck for
any of them, but they grin
when I do. You wanna have
some breakfast?

The charm comes off like cologne,
irresistibly persuasive.

. . . a little lobster on
the beach, I'm twenty minutes
away.

          KEMP
It sounds inviting, but I
gotta wait for the man.

> SANDERSON
> He isn't coming. Cancelled.

> KEMP
> That's not what it says on
> the board?

> SANDERSON
> It will in a minute, I just
> called Miami . . .

*As he says it the board confirms it
and SANDERSON grins.*

> SANDERSON
> Come and have some breakfast.
> I got a couple of things
> might interest you.

*Checking his watch KEMP reaches for
suitcase and camera.*

> KEMP
> I better call in.

> SANDERSON
> You can phone from the car.

24 EXT. WIDE OVER TROPICAL LANDSCAPE.
    DAY.

*Back in picture-postcard land. It's a
Rousseau painting except for the
road. A red Alpha Romeo with the
EVERLEY BROTHERS blaring descends
through silver mist to the
sea.*

25 EXT/INT. COUNTRY ROAD/ALPHA
    CONVERTIBLE. DAY.

*Crazy-looking cliffs soar out of
the foliage. Luxurious orchids and
screech of tropical birds. The landscape is totally unspoiled and with
so much beauty about it seems a
shame to cut into the car. But if
you've got to have one, what better
than a gleaming new Italian
convertible.*

*KEMP looks bewitched by it all but
pretends not to be impressed by the
radio-phone. Finishing his call he
hands it over and SANDERSON snaps
it back into place. They're both
playing games, but from opposite
sides of the fence.*

SANDERSON
(re. phone)
There's only two on the
island, maybe three.

*The engine sounds peachy, KEMP is
dazzled by the scenery.*

KEMP
No one told me it was so
pretty.

SANDERSON
God's idea of money.
(grinning)
You know what makes this
place a gold mine? Something
that doesn't exist.

KEMP
How's that?

SANDERSON
Land. There isn't enough of
it, and those who know how to
get it, get the gold.

*They may have already gone through
gates but now they're outside a
house. Crisp architecture and
swooning palms, it's what you might*

want to call art-concrete. SANDERSON
loses the car like a tossed hat and
KEMP follows inside.

26 INT. BEACH HOUSE/PRIVATE BEACH. DAY.

The back of the house is all view
of the ocean. Beyond is a private
beach with Rousseau either side and
twenty-five feet of brand-new yacht
out on the azure. This is no place
for the envious. Everything KEMP
sees he likes [envies] but the big
one doesn't hit until they walk out
onto the terrace. Fixing rum on ice
SANDERSON shouts down the beach. An
audit of the approaching girl is
unavoidable. Naked except for
jewellery and virtually transparent
sarong, she's a stunner [previously
believed to be a mermaid]. Making
introductions, SANDERSON brings
drinks.

                    SANDERSON
        Paul's joining us for break-
        fast that looks like it's
        gonna be a lunch.
                (kisses her)
        This is Chenault.

*Surprise to see each other and
attraction in equal measure.
SANDERSON gets a reading via his
impeccable radar.*

You two know each other?

*A definite no in CHENAULT's eyes,
and KEMP plays it OK.*

           KEMP
I thought we may have met on
the plane?

          CHENAULT
I don't think so, I flew boyfriend airlines.

*In a rather disconcerting way she
slips into high heels, and clearly
belongs to him like everything else
on show.*

You like lobster, Paul?

           KEMP
You know what, I might not
have time today. I didn't
realise the drive was gonna
take so long.

SANDERSON
How long have you got?

KEMP
In fifteen minutes, I'm late.

CHENAULT
I'll cut up a pineapple.

SANDERSON
    (after her)
. . . and you might want to
put on some clothes.
    (half smile)
She sunbathes in the nude,
and a few of the over-tanned
locals tend to treat it as a
tourist attraction.

KEMP
It doesn't surprise me . . .
I mean . . . in a tasteful
way . . .

SANDERSON
You mean, you'd like to fuck
her to a pulp . . . It's a
private beach . . . they
shouldn't be here. Sit down
. . . c'mon, Paul, sit down,
we'll get you a cab.

A choice of white-leather and
SANDERSON refreshes drinks. As KEMP
sits a dazzle comes from the floor.
It's a live tortoise, encrusted with
phoney diamonds. This creature and
Chenault share something in common.
Both get jewels and both are in situ,
and owned, to compliment SANDERSON.

                    SANDERSON
        His name's Harry, I got the
        idea from a book.
                (sitting)
        I wanted to talk because I'm
        looking for someone who can
        assimilate contradictory
        points of view, and make them
        into one voice.
                (the charm)
        You're a novelist, right?

                    KEMP
        Where'd you hear that?

                    SANDERSON
        Newspapers are full of gossip.
                (scooping HARRY)
        I'm looking for someone who's
        good with words. Next day you
        turn up, and coz I believe in
        good luck, I thought maybe

you were it? What I need is
someone with the right kind
of eyes.

                    KEMP
For looking at what?

                    SANDERSON
Looking at that . . .

*He gestures expansively at the
amazing and unspoiled view.*

27 INT. STAIRWAY. OLD BUILDING. SAN
    JUAN. DAY.

*Ancient stairs ascend into gloom. As
KEMP peers up from the hallway a heap
of flotsam crashes down the stair-
well, primarily cardboard and bundles
of newspaper. Midway up the stairs he
runs into SALA who struggles with a
sack of empty bottles and similar
refuse that couldn't be thrown.*

                    SALA
Hey . . . you made it . . .

*Rejecting a hand he disappears with
his clattering junk.*

BRUCE ROBINSON

SALA
It's right at the top.

28 INT. SALA'S APARTMENT. DAY.

*You can probably smell it before you
see it. KEMP lowers his suitcase and
begins to show himself around. The area
designated as kitchen exercises the
greatest pull. Much has been eaten in
here but little cleaned up. A goldfish
indulges a limited quality of life in
the only example of clean water. Apart
from an incongruous [brand-new] spin-
dryer for clothes, everything else is
comprehensively vile.*

*Degradation expands to engulf the
apartment, made claustrophobic with
photographs. Most walls are plastered
and many are crime-scene horrors.
Disturbing events are ubiquitous [a
head in a street catches Kemp's
eye]. The rest is threadbare and
thrift-store. A pair of armchairs
face the only window, though why
this should be so isn't clear.*

*Two rooms remain to be explored. He
heads for one when a cockerel crows
in another. Was it a cockerel? How*

can a cockerel be up here? KEMP
pushes at a bedroom door. The bed
was expected, but not a bunch of
cages on top of each other wherein
various live foul are resident.
One or two are swaddled head to foot
in bandage like balls of string.

KEMP closes the door on them, checks
out an antediluvian radio-gram and
its stack of records. Discovers
something of interest as SALA re-
appears, wasted and dripping sweat.

> SALA
> . . . was trying to get the
> place ship/shape before you
> arrived . . .

Detouring via a refrigerator he
hands KEMP a beer.

> Salut.

> KEMP
> *(re. record)*
> 'Adolph Hitler Speaks'?

> SALA
> Not mine . . . the Nazi
> stuff belongs to Moburg.

KEMP
Moburg lives here?

SALA
He keeps his uniform here. I
never see him, from one
month's end to the next . . .
    (selling it)
. . . you can see, it's
quite spacious? Don't look at
the kitchen . . . the water's
off, it's a problem in the
valve.

KEMP
I thought you had a TV?

SALA
I said, I kind of have a TV.

He gestures at the armchairs facing
the opposite building.

The guy across the alley has
a TV . . . I have binoculars.
    (finds them)
His wife's deaf, with the
window open, you hear every
word.

A terrible gurgling echoes in pipes and SALA is vindicated.

It's coming up.

                    KEMP
I noticed you have some chickens in the bedroom.

                    SALA
Cockerels. I'm sweating the grease out . . . Don't worry about them, they're moving to my room.

                    KEMP
What d'you do? Eat them?

                    SALA
Eat them?
         (drinks)
Nahh, I don't eat them . . .

29 EXT. COCKPIT. MOUNTAIN VILLAGE. DAY.

A pair of fighting cocks clash mid-air. A roar goes up from an encirclement of black faces. I could tell you about the blood and the dust and the feathers, but it'll read like half-assed Hemmingway. All I

*know is it's going to cost thousands
of feet of film to get this right.*

*The birds are an expression of arro-
gance, strutting like rock stars in
the insolence of their breed. No such
description applies to the frenzy of
spectators. Not a few are Mulatto, a
few more Black, but most are Jiberos
from the interior, harsh faces with
wild eyes and lousy teeth.*

*Every contorted face is subcon-
sciously fighting with the roosters,
winning, loosing, laughing and
cursing, shrieking in Spanish and
waving mangy dollar bills in new
bets.*

*SALA and KEMP are just about the
only white men. In the melee of
excitement and shifting smoke it's
suddenly over and SALA's cock has
won! Jubilation is shared with KEMP.*

> SALA
> On a trade wind, my boy.

*Money changes hands and like Jiberos
SALA administers first-aid to the
victor with his mouth, sucking and*

*spitting blood. Simultaneously the
ring is prepared for fresh
contenders. The dirt is raked and a
sign of the cross is scratched into
the floor. A pinch of holy dust is
rubbed into beaks of the combatants
and tethers released. Beady eyes
engage a paralysed stare, provoking
the first strike.*

You know something? If you
gave these guys the best food
on earth, but kept 'em tied,
they'd ignore the food and
stare at each other until
they starved to death.

*SALA has his money on a black and
gold, instantly engrossed as KEMP
finds interest elsewhere. He pushes
through the mob leaving Birds and
the Cariadors to get on with it.*

30 EXT. STREET. MOUNTAIN VILLAGE. DAY.

*Everything looks like two hundred
years ago. Starved horses and
barking dogs. A Catholic church up
the hill and poverty everywhere
else. Although its source isn't
clear, smoke hangs in the air with*

*a disagreeable odour. KEMP wanders
and might even take an occasional
photograph. Clutching precious birds,
more men and boys are on their way
to the fights. Strictly a male
affair, the women and girls take
what meagre advantage they can with
sad little stalls at the roadside.
Rattan is spread under trees where
you can buy seashell trinkets,
sugarcane, black tobacco, and rum.*

*A pair of ramshackle trucks full of
garbage trundle past, but KEMP is
looking at a MAN ON A HORSE.
Obviously a personage of some importance, he wears a red and yellow
bandanna tied like a turban with a
filthy Panama hat on top.*

*Either side of his saddle are cages,
one transporting the biggest fucking
chicken KEMP has ever seen. Except
this isn't a chicken of course, it's
a nightmare of a COCKEREL. A gang
of kids chase after the RIDER while
KEMP's attention returns to the
trucks. Belching exhaust they vanish
where the sky becomes asthma and
seagulls hover overhead.*

31 EXT. GARBAGE DUMP. NEAR VILLAGE. DAY.

The trucks dump their load and gulls celebrate their arrival. KEMP peers across a wasteland of putrescence, despoiling what was once a beautiful landscape. City filth stretches for as far as he cares to look. But his interest orientates around the imme-diate foreground. The sub-poor live here in hulks of American cars. Kids and dogs and cooking fires in the rat lands. To describe it as a shanty would invest it with a status. KEMP is genuinely moved to discover such deprivation. He takes the photograph of an exquisite child living in a rusted Chevrolet.

32 EXT. COCKPIT. VILLAGE. DAY

A COCKEREL crows in defiance above its vanquished enemy. It's the big chicken, the nine pound nightmare that arrived on horseback. It swag-gers the pit daring any punk hen to challenge it. At some point KEMP has reappeared.

> SALA
> . . . they call him, 'El

Monstruo', they say he's never
lost a fight in three years.
        (focusing KEMP)
Where have you been?

                KEMP
Looking around.

                SALA
C'mon, we're outta here.

*SALA dumps his chicken cage in
the back of the Fiat and shouts
in Spanish to a bunch of kids.
For a handful of coins they
agree to start the car. A moment
later SALA and KEMP are on
their way with a dozen children
pushing.*

33 INT. FIAT CONVERTIBLE/COUNTRY ROAD.
    DAY.

*The motor kicks in and they take
off in a cloud of dust. Cockerels
stare from the back, KEMP sorts out
the beers.*

SALA

I tell you, we were on a roll
till that thing turned up

KEMP
        (counting)
Two hundred and seventeen
dollars.

SALA

Not bad.

KEMP

Two hundred and seventeen dollars?
That's a shit-load of money?

SALA

Relatively a shit-load,
they're expensive to train.
        (drinks)
I've seen guys win two thousand, ten on North Beach.

KEMP

Ten thousand dollars? Why
don't he take 'El Monstruo'
down there?

SALA

You're talking the environs
of the Hilton Hotel . . .

they wear bow ties and shiny
shoes . . . there's no hook
for his kind of hat . . .

34 INT. (P.O.V. BINOCULARS) APARTMENT.
DAY.

*Massive close-up of RICHARD NIXON on
a black & white TV. He's partici-
pating in the so-called Great
Presidential Debates of 1960 and
lying about something or other. At
the other side of the debate is a
youthful J. F. KENNEDY, brimming
charm, and Dick can't compete. The
proceedings are adjudicated by a
sycophant with a crew-cut, his questions about as penetrating as an
assault with marshmallow.*

KEMP (O.S.)
How long can this blizzard of
shame go on? Look at this
asshole, besotted with his own
righteousness . . . 'Black is
a very dark shade of white',
well, thank you very much, Mr
Nixon . . .

*Both stare through binoculars. KEMP
first to lower them.*

I can't listen to any more of
this . . . he lies like he
breathes . . . Imagine
spending your entire life
lying . . .

*At some point KEMP gets to the
fridge and hauls out beer.*

Holy Christ, it never got
worse. The only eventuality
worse than him is you know
one day, some filthy whore-
beast will come along, and
make him look like a liberal.

*He sits at a portable typewriter,
papers and photographs.*

The only up side with Nixon
is he ain't gonna win.

SALA
He's got the grin.

                    KEMP
He ain't gonna win. The Irish
guy will win, but they'll
never let him live.

                    SALA
How do you know that?

                    KEMP
I do horoscopes . . .

*By now he's picked up where he left
it on the typewriter, shuffles notes
and Zippos a butt. Referencing
pictures taken at the garbage-dump,
he converts them into a burst of
words. SALA is back on the binoculars and it takes a while to realise
MOBURG has arrived. Dressed in
sandals and raincoat, he carries a
plastic sack into the kitchen, a
presence insisting itself, like a
low life Santa Claus.*

                    KEMP
I thought you said he never
came here?

                    SALA
He's got filters.

MOBURG is transferring the saturated content of his sack into the spin-dryer. KEMP follows SALA into the kitchen.

KEMP

What filters?

SALA

He goes over the wall at the Barcardi plant.

MOBURG

These filters are the last in line in the distillation process, they contain more ethanol than rocket-fuel.

Hence the brand-new spin-dryer. He closes the lid and extraction begins. It will end via a small tap at the bottom of the machine. In anticipation (and looking more and more like a freaked alchemist) MOBURG empties his pockets of bottles and used jam jars, crouching to fill the first.

KEMP

What's it like?

MOBURG
A hand on the brain. Off the
scale, it's 470 proof.

KEMP
There's no such thing as 470
proof alcohol.

MOBURG
A certainty you might be
required to moderate.
          (filling)
No smoking in the extraction
area, if you please.

KEMP
Don't be ridiculous.

*The wizard and his broth have
been challenged. A disturbing
sneer emerges. Stepping away MOBURG
takes a mouthful of brew and
striking a match puts fire up the
room like a flame-thrower on a tank.
KEMP is momentarily taken aback.*

MOBURG
Not for the social drinker.
          (proffering)
Wanna quaff?

KEMP

Not right now . . . I got a
deadline, I gotta write.

MOBURG corks a bottle for SALA,
suspicious eyes after KEMP.

MOBURG

Whass he writing?

SALA

He's lifting the stone on the
American Dream . .

Reseating at the typewriter, KEMP
waves a wad of pictures.

KEMP

Guayanilla Bay.

MOBURG

Oh, yeah, it's bad up there.
          (KEMP types)
You might find such a topic
attracts a limited readership.

KEMP

I only need one.
          (snubs butt)
I'm taking it into Lotterman.

MOBURG

Did I hear someone say, 'Good
Luck'? I went there this
morning, and he unfired me on
a 'temporary basis', maggot
that he is . . . I'd like to
take something into Lotterman,
like a slide-action, fuck-you
gun.

SALA

Don't drink that here.

MOBURG

Just a nipperoo, old boy,
quality test.

He takes a substantial hit, gets
back to killing Lotterman.

. . . slow-motion murder,
like they do in the movies
. . . see him flying backwards, fucking arms flapping
in the air 'OK, mother, look
upon the last face you see
this side of hell.' Bam! Down
he goes, morsels of vital
organ spinning away into slow-
motion flesh orbit . . . Bam!
There goes his asshole . . .

Bam! There goes his dick
. . . Bam! Bam! Fuck you,
Lotterman, you're in a
B-Fucking Movie, and I am the
Death-Machine.

*He has become psychotically drunk,
and the others alarmed.*

Shall we have some Adolph?

                    KEMP
Definitely not.

                    SALA
On your way, Moburg, we're
expecting quests.

                    MOBURG
You said he was writing a book.

                    KEMP
I said I was writing an
essay, and it requires some
shut-mouth.

                    MOBURG
Don't waste your time with
junk-yard losers . . .
          (swilling brew)
. . . this country was built

on genocide and slavery . . .
We killed all the black guys
who were here, then shipped
in new black guys of our own
. . . then we brought Jesus
in like a bar of soap . . .

                    SALA
Let's go.

                    MOBURG
You know it . . . I am the
religious correspondent.

*MOBURG seems unaware SALA is
hassling him through the door. The
CAMERA corkscrews from above as he
descends the stairs.*

. . . fuck off with your
Jesus police . . . If the
Bible's God's book, why
didn't he give it to
everyone?

35 INT. LOTTERMAN'S OFFICE. DAILY STAR.
NIGHT.

*The corkscrewing visual continues.
Starting close on a sheet of typed
manuscript, it expands to include*

*the man reading it. The air is
filled with cigar smoke and
it's clearly very late. LOTTERMAN
licks a forefinger to turn a
page and looks up. The camera has
arrived at KEMP who sits at the
opposite side of the desk smoking
in expectation.*

LOTTERMAN
. . . 'we give more money to
parking meters than we do to
kids to eat . . .'

KEMP
Don't read me like that, I've
done the research.

*Another twelve pages of it.
LOTTERMAN looks over his glasses.*

. . . a twelve-thousand-
ton rust-bucket went down
in the bay, full of hydro-
chloric acid . . . it
killed everything in the
sea, killed off the
fishermen, their kids are
picking garbage . . .

LOTTERMAN

Don't get angry, it's hot
outside . . . you want a
Scotch?

*Sure he does and LOTTERMAN pours
them and reseats himself.*

Ten years ago, five years
ago, I may have said, go
after it. Now I say, go with
it, there's nothing you can
change . . . Sometimes you
just gotta spew over the
side, and keep rowing . . .

KEMP

Into a nut-brown sunset?

LOTTERMAN

We are in a land of multiple
outrage . . . thousands
trodden on before you wake up
for breakfast . . .
       (swallows Scotch)
That isn't 'news', it's a
commercial reality, and
providing it isn't their
sunset, no one gives one
fifth of a fuck.

KEMP
You underestimate your
readers.

LOTTERMAN
I don't think so.

KEMP
You underestimate me. You told
me, make it work, and that's
what I wanna do . . . wind
down this La Zonga crap, and
make a newspaper.

LOTTERMAN
Let me tell you some home
truth. This paper has been on
its knees to a bank since the
day it opened. Like almost
every newspaper on earth it's
financed by its advertising.
Without advertising, not only
is there no 'La Zonga',
there's no newspaper to write
it in . . . thus, there are
one or two things we don't
write about.

KEMP
In other words, nothing at all?

LOTTERMAN

In one other word, 'discretion'.
    (elbows)
You are not a foreign
correspondent in some far-
flung foreign land, this is
America . . .

KEMP

This is Puerto Rico.

LOTTERMAN

This is *America*. You think a
plumber from Normal Illinois
saves for twenty-five years
to come here on a cruise ship
to read about bad times on
the sugar plantations? They
don't give a fuck.
    (didactic smile)
The average guy don't rock the
boat coz he wants to climb
aboard it and our readership
is vividly average. They don't
wanna know who the losers are,
they wanna know who *won*. Who
won the bowls, who won the
races, who won the pot on the
slot-machine? Look at me, Kemp,
you are not sleeping, you are

wide-awake, and this is the American Dream.

He hits the Scotch in one, retrieves his essay and stands.

                    KEMP
There's so many hotels, you
can't see the sea.

                    LOTTERMAN
You can see the sea by
checking into the hotels.

                    KEMP
Pay to see the sea.

                    LOTTERMAN
What's the matter with that?
You're paying to be in the
Dream. It's a thin veneer,
Kemp, between the Dream and
the Reality . . . Wake
them up, and people might
start asking for their money
back.

KEMP heads for the door, tearing his manuscript as he goes.

KEMP
You're the boss.

LOTTERMAN
Not quite . . .

By now the pages are confetti, fall
like it as KEMP exits.

. . . the editorial policy of
this newspaper is owned by
the Dream . . .

And swooning violins [like canned
Mantovani] dissolve into a dazzling
sea like it might be a dream. Amongst
the light are a pair of silhouettes.
Naked in waist-deep water, they cling
together, her legs wound round his
hips and her arms around his neck.
Her head is thrown backwards and her
hair drenches the water, like someone
actually caught a mermaid.

36 EXT. SEASCAPE/TERRACE. BEACH HOUSE.
    DAY.

SANDERSON and CHENAULT are making
love in the sea. Nobody should be
looking and maybe KEMP wishes he
wasn't. But he is, and can't stop

*himself. Clutching a bunch of
flowers, he's obviously just arrived
on the terrace. A rush of emotions
are instant [embarrassment, jeal-
ously, and fascination]. The latter
momentarily insists and he watches
transfixed, although finally it's
jealousy that turns away.*

*Retreating to the living room, he
looks about for anything as good to
look at. Sees the encrusted tortoise
and tells it to scram. His interest
turns yet again to a tall brass
telescope on a tripod. Maybe he'll
take just another peek?*

*P.O.V. as the telescope comes into
focus. It briefly passes the
anchored yacht before discovering
the lovers. This close it's almost
unbearable. CHENAULT is reclining on
the ocean as SANDERSON gives it to
her. With arms outstretched like
wings, she arches her back and KEMP
is almost disabled with lust, 'Oh,
God, don't do that. How could you
do that?'*

*Lascivious commentary continues as
KEMP imposes his own emotional take*

on the proceedings. Suddenly he jerks his eye away and clutches his face, 'Ah, Ah, Ah.' It's too much to bear but too much to miss, and he goes in for another view.

SANDERSON stands on the yacht pulling CHENAULT out of the water. He gets into swimming shorts and she her bikini, attending to the bra between kisses. 'Oh, my God, will you look at that?' Meanwhile a middle-aged couple have arrived via the hall. I'll get to describe them when there's time.

> KEMP
> (*spying*)
> You are so bad/sweet . . .
> ahhh . . .

> MRS ZIMBURGER
> Hal?

KEMP whips around and stares at them like they stare at him.

> KEMP
> I'm a friend of Hal's. I was looking at his. Boat.

ZIMBURGER
She's a sweet little beauty
. . . you been aboard?
(he hasn't)
Great little island hopper.

MRS ZIMBURGER
We've all been down on her,
it's a wonderful experience.

37 EXT. SHORELINE. PRIVATE BEACH. DAY.

SANDERSON exits the sea with a
spear-gun and CHENAULT follows with a
sack of lobsters. Both seem delighted
to see KEMP. He and ZIMBURGER have
sauntered down to greet them.

SANDERSON
You guys are early . . .
(shaking hands)
Did you meet?

KEMP
We got first names.

SANDERSON
Art Zimburger, late of the
U.S. Marines, great friend of
mine . . . this is Mr Paul
Kemp, of the New York Times.

ZIMBURGER
You're the writer?

CHENAULT
Paul's a novelist.

KEMP
That kind of thing.

Off they all walk towards the house,
ZIMBURGER escorted by CHENAULT.
Legs and legs and TITS and LEGS and
KEMP doesn't look. Puts an aside to
SANDERSON as they walk behind.

KEMP
New York Times?

SANDERSON
He don't know one from the
other . . . just go with it
. . . this guy is key . . .

KEMP
Key to what?

SANDERSON
Key to the discussion we're
about to have . . .
        (spots them)
Look at those mothers . . .

*He refers to some SWARTHY FACES
hidden in the undergrowth.*

Come with me, Kemp.

*Sucked along in the wake of anger
KEMP finds himself part of the
confrontation. Two of the faces have
already gone, but one remains to
defy SANDERSON. He's a brutal-
looking bastard in his twenties, good
looks spoiled by a deep scar on his
cheek. Clearly this isn't simply
about spying on the Yanquis, it's
about resentment at the white man's
presence.*

This is a private beach.

*The INTRUDER stands his ground,
staring acid at the Yanks.*

INTRUDER
We are not on it.

SANDERSON
Yeah, but we are, and what we
do is private.

The INTRUDER alternates his contempt between the white men.

> SANDERSON (COND)
> Now get the fuck gone.

Reeking animosity the Puerto Rican finally decides to walk.

> If I see your face again, you gonna have a 12-gauge shotgun telling you what to do.

38 INT. LIVING ROOM/TERRACE. BEACH HOUSE. DUSK.

A blood-red sunset outside, candles already lit in here. SANDERSON sports casual silk and plays the impeccable host. Several guests have arrived, Golden Mariners, on their way to 'meet the yacht in St Lucia'. There's a lot of tan and perfume about, unlikeable music on the stereo and conversation oiled by booze. CHENAULT is in and out of her guests delivering top-ups from a pitcher of white rum. She wears white heels and the kind of scant dress revered by wankers.

Despite his entrapment in conversation, she's a magnet for KEMP. He takes every opportunity to look at her. And is it a delusion that she seems just as often looking at him?

The ZIMBURGERS are a pair of reactionary twats. One uses a grin and the other doesn't. MRS ZIMBURGER has a budget lift and lipstick on excessively white teeth. ZIMBURGER is wasted on rum and until CHENAULT arrives with more, it doesn't matter whether we hear the yelling bastard or not.

ZIMBURGER
. . . if ever there was a kingdom of Satan, the Soviet Union is it . . . there's only one way you come to terms with Communism, and that is to destroy it, hit it before it hits us, in a devastating democratic strike . . .

Lunging across his wife he directs his invective at KEMP.

> . . . they need a guy to
> press the button? I am that
> man.

*Fragments of masticated pistachio
accompany the diatribe. CHENAULT
tops up the glasses. A discreet
whisper to KEMP.*

CHENAULT
You need rescuing?

MRS ZIMBURGER
Don't take him away, he's
very entertaining.
    (gets a refill)
We were discussing Cuba, but
kind of veered off.
    (swallows it)
Paul presents us with a somewhat 'liberal' point of view.

ZIMBURGER
There's no such thing as a
liberal . . . a liberal is a
Communist with a college
education, thinking negro
thoughts . . .

*SANDERSON is at the front door
greeting new arrivals. ZIMBURGER*

finishes his tirade before getting up to join them.

. . . and here's a fact for
you, 76.4 per cent of
negros are controlled from
Moscow . . .

                    MRS ZIMBURGER
Why Castro gets an easy ride.

                    ZIMBURGER
. . . in my view we should
bomb Cuba off the face of the
earth and let its people live
in peace . . .

*Off he goes following into hand-
shakes. SEGURRA has arrived with a
sixty-five-year-old Hispanic in
sunglasses and a thousand-dollar
suit. SANDERSON escorts them all
out to the terrace where cigars are
lit and sliding doors closed.*

                    KEMP
Who's that?

                    CHENAULT
Segurra's daddy . . . it's
who you're waiting for.

He's more interested in her and it's difficult not to be. Filling his glass she sits on the arm of the sofa. Pure sex in a lot of proximity and no question putting it out.

Thank you for the roses.

KEMP
I didn't think you noticed?

She's utterly intoxicating, red lips in a whispering pout.

CHENAULT
Of course I noticed.

He's right inside her perfume. Lips close enough to kiss. It's a moment of promise and risk and sudden interruption.

SANDERSON
Paul, would you come in here?

CHENAULT slides into the sofa where he just sat. Watches the terrace doors close on handshakes before they all sit.

39 EXT. TERRACE. BEACH HOUSE. DUSK.

*LOUIS MUNOZ SEGURRA doesn't have
to contribute to be centre of
discussions. What he says goes, and
he doesn't need to say anything.
It's his son and SANDERSON who talk
the talk.*

SEGURRA

Let me just start by saying
this is a purely informal
meeting, and incidentally, you
don't worry about Lotterman.

ZIMBURGER

Lotterman?
        (surprise)
What's Lotterman got to do
with the *New York Times*?

SANDERSON
        (covering)
Mr Kemp subs for a variety of
newspapers, occasionally
writes for the *Star* . . .
What he does in his spare
time is his affair . . .

KEMP

That's how I like it.

SEGURRA
We'd like you to do some
writing for us.

KEMP
So I gather. About what?

SANDERSON
In a sentence, we wanna set
something up and have the
public as our friends? And
there are various ways we can
do that.
             (charm on auto)
Let me tell you how this kind
of thing works, Paul. Suppose
by way of example, you wanted
to put up taxes by five
per cent? The smart way of
doing it, is to float the
idea of a ten per cent hike?
Let them all shout about it,
get themselves in a fuss?
Then you offer 'concessions',
how about seven per cent? No
way, they will say. All
right, let's stay friends,
and make a compromise at
five? Bingo . . . they think
they won something, and you've

got the five per cent you
wanted in the first place.

                    SEGURRA
The same thing applies to
real estate. You wanna build
five houses, put in a planning application for *fifty*.

                    KEMP
How many do you want to build?

                    SEGURRA
None.
          (gets to it)
We want to build one hotel.

                    KEMP
So what's the deal with that?
(KEMP hardly bothers a shrug.)
Looking around this place, I
don't think anyone'll notice?

                    SEGURRA
It isn't in this place . . .

                    SANDERSON
. . .it's an island, sensi-
tive for a variety of reasons
we don't want to get into
now. Nobody wants a paradise

                    — 106 —

choked with hotels, but everybody will be pleased to
compromise at one . . .

SEGURRA
. . . this is going to
require some clever writing
in various carefully placed
articles . . .

*KEMP looks at faces looking at him,
it begins to look iffy.*

KEMP
Isn't that kind of thing illegal?

ZIMBURGER
If I may say so, Mr Kemp, that
is an inappropriate question.

KEMP
Where's the island?

SANDERSON
Can't tell you. Not yet.

SEGURRA
Discretion is paramount, if
you join us, you'll need to
sign some papers.

*The door is already on the slide,
CHENAULT puts a smile in.*

CHENAULT
There's a man outside in a
funny little car for Paul.

KEMP
(standing)
Oh, yeah . . . I didn't
realise it was so late . . .

CHENAULT
You can't stay? The mermaids
come out in moonlight?

*Meaning some fun in the ocean? He
gets handshakes instead.*

SANDERSON
You don't have to come to any
decision now, Paul, and I
fully understand any reserva-
tions you may have . . .

SEGURRA
. . . we have a meeting on
Monday in Hal's office . . .
If you wanna be part of what
will be a very exciting
project, come along.

40 INT/EXT. FIAT CONVERTIBLE/JUNGLE
   ROAD. NIGHT.

*Yellow light from the wireless. A
pointer scans channels for a
station. But it's all Spanish trash
or Connie Francis so she wins it.
The headlights are like candles on a
spooky jungle road. SALA drives with
his cockerels on the back seat. He's
annoyed because they're lost and
KEMP is no help. He's too drunk to
think of anything but Chenault.*

> KEMP
>
> From the moment we met I knew
> there was going to be some-
> thing between us . .

> SALA
>
> It's called her fiancée . . .

*A reality KEMP can't face and he
all but writhes in agony.*

> KEMP
>
> Oh, God, I'm so hopelessly
> and progressively in love.

> SALA
>
> Do not confuse love with lust

nor drunkenness with judge-
ment.

He's forced to stop the car. A
swamp steams in headlights.

What other ideas do you have
in respect of navigation?

KEMP
I said, straight down the
street and turn left.

SALA
We already are straight down
the street, and there is no
left . . . it's a swamp . . .

KEMP
All right, back up . . .
          (backing up)
How were the fowl?

SALA
A public humiliation, the
bastards disgraced me.

Reverse finds another dirt road.
SALA shoves it into gear.

KEMP

You never realise the genius
of some of these love songs
until you're smitten?

SALA

You want my advise?

KEMP

If it involves her, no.

SALA

Stay away from her, and stay
away from Sanderson, you're
way out of your depth.

KEMP

I got no brief for Sanderson,
or his pissy rip-off island. I
just want some apple blossom,
lipstick, and fucks . . .

SALA

You are in total denial, she's
fucking someone else, and as I
understand it, about to be
married to him.

KEMP
        (hands over ears)
Ah, ah, ah, ah!

SALA
You won't even make an
invite.
    (violent stop)
I don't believe this, we are
back where we started.

*Coloured lights about fifty yards
down a dirt road. A shot-up sign
reads 'Cafe Cabrones', and SALA
points in exasperation.*

That's the same Cabrones we
passed ten minutes ago.

*Slumping back he punches the
steering wheel. Reaches for a
flagon. He takes a breathtaking swig
and shoves it across.*

We need directions.

*KEMP hits it and a noise comes from
his throat. Something like cold
water suddenly introduced to a
boiled-dry kettle.*

Let's get in there and get
something to eat.

                    KEMP
    No.
            (trying to breathe)
    No.

                    SALA
    I haven't spent all day on a
    beach, munching lobster with
    criminals, and I'm starving.

41 EXT. DINING TERRACE. CAFE
    CABRONES. NIGHT.

    *A couple of strings of blue lights
    and a bunch of dirty old palms.
    Sand on boards, trash out of a
    jukebox, and the dynamic isn't
    friendly. Smoke loiters with nowhere
    to go, just like Jiberos at the
    bar. No white faces, and the Yanks
    attract head turns as the only
    Gringos. Subsequent to seating, a
    GIRL with an ass the size of a
    wrecking-ball presents herself as
    waitress. Nobody sober would ever
    ask her for food.*

                    SALA
    Two beers, two rums, one
    steak.

                    GIRL
The kitchen is closed.

                    KEMP
All right, two beers, two
rums.

                    SALA
And one steak.

                    GIRL
Cerrado, mister.

                    SALA
Yeah, but let's not bother me
with that? You got a sign
up here saying Food till
Midnight, and I want a
steak.

*All but sneering she thumps off with
SALA'S eyes in pursuit.*

A Girl of the Swamp . . .
and that reminds me, we need
a map.

*KEMP raises the brim of his Panama
revealing parboiled eyes.*

KEMP

You know what, we're drinking
too much rum.

SALA

There's no other way.

KEMP

I'm getting double ashtray
and a double salt-pot.

SALA

You got a Moburg bi-focal.

KEMP

Christ, this is heinous.
        (one eye)
Imagine what it must be like
to be an alcoholic.

*More alcohol arrives delivered
by a man in a greasy apron.
It's clearly his place and
these boys ain't welcome in
it.*

PATRON

Two dollars.
        (drinks down)
You pay and you go.

SALA

I don't see a steak?

PATRON

No steak.

SALA

What do you mean, no steak?

KEMP

I think he means, no steak.

PATRON

The kitchen is closed. I got
no way of serving you.

SALA

Listen, you don't wanna hear
about my bad day, and I don't
want no graveside out of you.
        (posturing)
If you can't cook it, bring
it like it is and I'll eat
it raw.

PATRON

Two dollars. You pay and go.

SALA

Don't bother me.

— 116 —

PATRON
You pay *now* or I call the
cops.

SALA
If you have no intention of
serving me steak, why don't
you do your best to fuck
off?

The PATRON retreats to his bar
where sympathetic ears wait to hear.
SALA has his back to them and KEMP
gets the view.

KEMP
It seems to me there's a bad
vibe developing . . .

The number of young Jiberos around
the bar has mysteriously multiplied
with incremental possibilities of
group violence.

. . . there's one or two
oddities giving us the eye . . .

SALA
Don't get paranoid.

                    KEMP
He's on the phone . . .

                    SALA
For what? Ordering food in
a restaurant . . . Let's
hope he's through to the
FBI.
          (noticing it)
what's the matter with you,
what are you smiling at?

*It's a paralysed shiteater through
which he manages to talk.*

                    KEMP
I'm not smiling, I'm main-
taining a casual face . . .
          (here's why)
A guy just walked in who has
good reason for regarding us
in a negative light.

                    SALA
Us?

                    KEMP
Me, and he's just seen me. He
wants revenge on the white man.

> SALA
>
> The fuck are you talking
> about?

He turns and is taken aback by the
cluster of hostile faces.

> KEMP
>
> How about the one with the
> dent?

No mistaking the one with the dent.
Staring with a psychotic eye it's
the BRUTE WITH THE SCAR threatened
by Sanderson.

> SALA
>
> The one with the eye?

> KEMP
>
> The very same.

> SALA
>
> Do we walk or run?

> KEMP
>
> Walk. I'll push the car.

By now both are smiling and stand,
avoiding the ONE WITH THE EYE. But
what about the drinks? KEMP has

*nothing and SALA not much more. He
makes it clear the birds cleaned him
out.*

Let's walk and hope he's
happy.

*Leaving a pile of pennies they prom-
enade towards the carpark.*

42 EXT. CARPARK/DIRT TRACK. NIGHT.

*Sultry darkness with fireflies and
fog. SALA is doing approximately one
mile an hour. He sits at the wheel
while KEMP pushes the Fiat in soft
sand. At a point approaching death
from asphyxiation the clutch jolts
in and the engine fires.*

*Gasping for air KEMP makes it to a
door. Simultaneously a shower of
pennies hit the car accompanied by
some emotional language in Spanish.
You don't need to look but the
PATRON is backed by various Jiberos
including the ONE WITH THE EYE.*

PATRON
Espurio . . . Bastard
yanquies . . . you think

bastards drink free in Puerto
Rico . . .

*Black muscle and eyes reeking
animosity. Is that the glint of a
machete? This is developing into one
of those cliches that is actually
happening. It's time to bid a gentle
farewell before these low-life-
looking ingrates tear them apart.*

43 INT. FIAT CONVERTIBLE/JUNGLE ROAD.
NIGHT.

*Five hundred cubic centimeters of
clapped-out engine plunge them into
an otherwise silent night. As they
reach the end of the track SALA
switches eyes to the mirror, hoping
against hope.*

> SALA
> Don't let me see headlights
> . . . please don't let me
> see headlights . . .
> *(a flare)*
> I've just seen headlights . . .

> KEMP
> Put your foot down.

> SALA
>
> Where exactly d'you think I've
> got it?

*Flat out and about as fast as a
roller-skate, the Fiat is no
competition for the car behind. It's
a monster convertible from the early
fifties, four or five yelpers on
board, swilling from the bottle and
poised for fun. It's traditional
stuff, bumping interspersed with
threatening headlights. Then the big
Ford overtakes and someone throws a
jack-handle through the Fiat's wind-
shield. Glass everywhere and SALA
looses it.*

> SALA
>
> We're gonna be killed,
> We're gonna be killed.

*Now in front, the Ford brakes like a
mother and sends everything spinning
to avoid it. The lights and tyres
and insanity are suddenly all in
reverse. One of the fighting Cocks
is out [and you can believe me or
believe me not] but it's perched on
top of SALA's head. Round and round
in circles they go. Crazy faces and*

*homicidal screeches. Empty beer
bottles rain down on the Fiat at
every passing opportunity.*

> SALA (COND)
> Get ready to run . . . run
> in opposite directions . . .

*By some process of centrifugal chaos
the Fiat is once again in front.
The ONE WITH THE EYE is waving a
machete and the Ford is alongside
like these maniacs are preparing to
board.*

> KEMP
> Gimme the Brew . . .
> (standing)
> Gimme the fucking Brew . . .

*The flagon finds itself in KEMP's
hand with a Zippo in the other. He
swigs a mouthful and spews out a
shocking lance of flame. Not so
funny in the Ford but delight in
the Fiat at the weapon's success.
Twisting in circles they deliver
another dose. A kaleidoscope of
fire and madness. KEMP is drunk and
astonishingly enjoying himself.
He's got it down and works the*

Brew and his Zippo in perfect synchronisation.

> KEMP (COND)
> Ha Ha Ha . . .

SALA wrestles the wheel like a mariner in a storm. It's a merry-go-round of panic and bad craziness and the cockerel is still on his head. All he sees is flame and blue light, and nobody saw the police van arrive. A sideways shunt and the Jiberos clamber the Fiat like ants on an apple. Trying to shake them off SALA spins it before some really bad news. The engine stalls inviting a conglomerate of knuckle-dusters, switch-blades and enraged faces.

First up gets full fry . . .

KEMP douses the bastards with flaming Brew. The ONE WITH THE EYE ducks but the one behind him doesn't. It's a COPPER in uniform with a hat now comprehensively on fire. The fire ball doesn't do a lot for his moustache nor stimulate benevolence from those accompanying him. The bad guys evaporate and

KEMP and SALA become recipients of official fury. Billy-clubs beat them out of the car followed by some select footwork. The last thing KEMP sees is an approaching black boot.

44 INT. COP STATION/COURT HOUSE. SAN JUAN. NIGHT.

Intermittent flashing blue-light on the police van. It arrives outside the station and escorts its cargo up the steps. SALA and KEMP are hand-cuffed, the latter almost unconscious.

A flash-bulb pops but you can't really see the faces beyond.

45 INT. HOLDING CELL. COURT HOUSE. NIGHT.

A steaming compost of humanity, about sixty in a cell built for six. Dreadful coincidentals of reality coincide with wake up for KEMP.

Blood mats his hair, and generally fucked up. The first face he sees belongs to a BLACK SAILOR from the Condado Toilets. Smudged lipstick and stubble through stale Max Factor. But he definitely likes KEMP, although he's the last thing you need with a headache from hell.

> SAILOR
> So what little wickedness puts you out of sorts with the world?
> *(who are you?)*
> My name's Auntie Mable.

Faces like fish in sardine oil, one of them belongs to SALA.

> SALA
> . . . we had a small piece of luck . . . I saw Moburg . . . at least, I think he saw us . . .

> A SHOUT
> What is this, fucking Belson?

KEMP is too busted to remember what happened and may say so.

> SALA
> . . . they got some kind of night-court going . . .

SAILOR
You on the sugar-train, honey,
the justice according to rum.

46 INT. COURTHOUSE. SAN JUAN. NIGHT.

A crumbling remnant from Colonial
Spain. Ceiling fans and unpleasant
neon. The JUDGE wears shades and
might not be sober. An acid-looking
POLICEMAN is presently on his feet
reading aloud in Spanish. The
charges are formidable and it seems
he wants these dangerous Yanks
locked up for ever.

KEMP and SALA are guilty, if only
by appearance. Both are handcuffed,
filthy and bleeding, archetypal
representatives of the low-life
characterising this place. But it's
even worse than that. SALA (in the
middle) is also handcuffed to some
anonymous DRUNK who has nothing to
do with their case. For the most
part he hangs forward semi-comatose
and it would seem the cops included
him by mistake. KEMP doesn't understand a word, forcing SALA to
whisper a surreptitious translation.

SALA

He says, we were animals on a
rampage of drunken anarchy
. . . poured gasoline on one
of his cops . . .

The Cop in question stands to adver-
tise his damage. A charred uniform
and a bald head minus moustache tell
the story.

SALA

Oh my God, we're doomed.

Next on the stand is the PATRON
from Carbones. Once again in Spanish,
he waves arms and emotes like he's
auditioning for some kind of opera.
Fist shaking at the defendants, it
seems they are guilty of everything
except raping his chef.

JUDGE

You have something to say?

SALA

Yes, your honour, I do.
Firstly, this guy handcuffed
to me, I never seen in my
life. Second, we'd like a
translation of the charges.

                    JUDGE
You heard what they said?

                    SALA
With respect, I heard people
speaking Spanish.

                    JUDGE
What kind of language do you
think we speak in this
country, mister?

The DRUNK vomits over the
side of the box like it's a
boat.

                    KEMP
He's not with us.

                    SALA
The cops attached him to get
a conviction.

                    JUDGE
          (ignoring him)
Did you leave the Cafe
Cabrones without paying?

By now the DRUNK has collapsed,
dragging SALA down with him.

Did you set fire to the
police officer, yes or no?

KEMP
Unfortunately he put himself
in the way of our flame . . .

SALA
      (half up)
That's right. No way did we
pour gasoline on his head and
laugh as we did it . . . it
wasn't like he said . . .

JUDGE
'Like he said'? Like you say,
you don't speak Spanish?

SALA
      (caught out)
Mr Kemp doesn't speak Spanish.

JUDGE
He will have plenty of opportunity to learn.
      (here it is)
The charges against you are
grave. Resisting arrest
carries a tariff alone of one
year in prison, never mind
assault with a deadly weapon.

The ancillary defendant farts like
everything in a farmyard.

I am going to refer this case
to a higher court, meanwhile
I remand you both in custody
for thirty days.

The gravel is about to crash down
when a voice makes itself heard from
the back of the court. It's
SANDERSON asking if he can have a
word? It isn't clear if the JUDGE
knows who he is, but an official
whispers in his ear and now he does.

Go ahead, Mr Sanderson.

                    SANDERSON
Thank you, Your Honour.
          (moving forward)
It isn't my purpose to inter-
rupt proceedings, but if the
intention is to remand these
two gentlemen, I would
respectfully ask for a brief
recess to allow me to contact
their Council.

                    JUDGE
Who is who?

SANDERSON
Alfredo Quinones.

*We don't know who Quinones is. But
the JUDGE clearly does.*

SANDERSON
It would necessitate getting
him out of bed, of course,
but given the importance of
these gentlemen to various
interests, I'm sure he would
be pleased as I to come down
here at three o'clock in the
morning?
(you dig?)
Perhaps we could have just a
minute or two, in private?

47 EXT. COURTHOUSE. SAN JUAN. NIGHT.

*The very first sense of dawn
over the architecture. SANDERSON
climbs into his Alpha. SALA and
MOBURG are coming down the steps of
the courthouse. But KEMP is the
first to arrive.*

KEMP
How much did we cost him?

MOBURG
Thousand dollars apiece.

KEMP
(to SANDERSON)
I can't thank you enough.

SANDERSON
(the smile)
Don't be late.

Shoving the car into gear he takes
off into silent streets.

48   INT. SALA'S APARTMENT. DAY.

A cockerel crows up a new day. Birds
are going off all over the flat.
Motoring on bile KEMP emerges from a
bedroom and makes it to the kitchen
on one eye. This is patently a hangover of great significance. Stiff
from the beating and suffering almost
total dehydration he goes for the
taps. Gets a gurgling in the pipes
but no water. Such a circumstance
offers scant debate and he all but
drinks the goldfish bowl dry.

Simultaneously an agonised plaint
rents air, 'Mother of Balls!'

followed by SALA. Like KEMP he's half dressed and monumentally hungover, but focused on a different priority.

> SALA
> We got to rescue the car.

Tearing the fridge open he slakes thirst with a can of beer.

> KEMP
> Not now, we'll do it later. I got a meeting.

> SALA
> We do not have later. They already had it twelve hours. I know how these bastards work.
> *(dressing)*
> They can strip a train to axles in twelve minutes. We'll be lucky to find an oil spot.

49 INT. TAXI. OUT OF TOWN. DAY.

KEMP and SALA are back of the Buick on a rough country road. Every bump adds new dimension to KEMP's headache. Plus the DRIVER

favours a station they hate but are
too wasted to get switched off. Hats
and shades and SALA has a stash of
beer.

                    KEMP
How long is this gonna take?

                    SALA
How would I know?

                    KEMP
I can't be late.

                    SALA
I don't know why you're going
at all. That guy is bad
company, a manipulative prick.

                    KEMP
Manipulated us outta jail,
didn't he?

                    SALA
Oh, sure.

Trumpets blare on the radio, SALA
gives direction in Spanish.

And now he fucking owns us.

KEMP
I got a tongue. Like a towel.

SALA
Want a beer?

KEMP
Do I want a beer? No, I do
not. I am never gonna touch
alcohol again.

50 EXT. JUNGLE ROAD. MIDDLE OF
NOWHERE. DAY.

*The cab pulls away, shifting
interest to KEMP before passing to
SALA. He moves towards the Fiat
with escalating anxiety.*

SALA
What Fresh Hell is this?

*Things are bad but not as bad as
they seem. The valve radio has
gone as have both the doors.
Why anyone would steal the doors
off a Fiat 500 is a question
without an answer. Worse is theft
of the seats. Both have vanished
leaving fresh air between the*

steering wheel and back seat. This
one has been left, but no doors and
no seats make the car look undriv-
able.

> KEMP
>
> That's a write-off, isn't it?

SALA takes affront at the sugges-
tion. The engine and wheels are
there. All they need is something to
sit on to drive it back. Before
such details are confronted, they
need to make sure it starts. SALA
gets in and tries kneeling to
operate the clutch. This isn't going
to work. He reverses himself like a
surfboard. With head and shoulders
on the rear seat he can just about
get a foot on the clutch.
Notwithstanding the hangover KEMP
pushes and the engine sputters into
life.

> KEMP
>
> I sense disaster.

> SALA
>
> You know what, I got a bril-
> liant idea . . .

51 EXT. COUNTRY INTERSECTION/MAIN
   ROAD. DAY.

   *A truck passes heading for the city.
   The Fiat pulls on to the main road.
   In any other automobile this wouldn't
   work, but the 500 is a very tiny
   car: SALA sits on the back seat with
   KEMP sitting on his lap. By this
   means they are able to progress like
   a normal vehicle.*

52 EXT. SUBURBS. SAN JUAN. DAY.

   *Wide over the streets but getting
   closer. Trailing exhaust the Fiat
   joins a flow of traffic heading into
   the old city.*

53 INT. FIAT CONVERTIBLE/BOULEVARD.
   DAY.

   *All in all this is going rather
   well. Except it isn't staying that
   way. A suspicious grating sound
   develops somewhere.*

                    KEMP
      What's that?

> SALA

Too much weight on the axle,
try and sit forward.

*KEMP hunches closer to the steering
wheel and SALA hangs on like a
pillion on a motorcycle. A shift of
weight has the desired effect. Less
groan as they approach traffic
lights.*

> KEMP

I'm gonna be late, I'm gonna
be a week late.

*Lights change and off they go again.
KEMP notices a subtle change in the
dynamic of his seating. Slowly at
first, but definitely happening,
SALA undulates like he's making
love.*

> KEMP

What are you doing, Sala?

> SALA

I suddenly realise how much I
like you. What d'you mean, 'what
am I doing?' There's something
wrong with the axle . . .

And with every yard it's getting worse, cranking SALA up and down like the proverbial fiddler's elbow. The Fiat is dying and they would almost certainly abandon it were it not for a black and white Police Cruiser that just appeared along side.

From the police point of view they've got a wrecked car with no doors and men engaged in sexual deviance. SALA recognises the face with the missing moustache.

> SALA
>
> Oh my God, it's the cop we set on fire.

> KEMP
>
> Try and look normal.

By now SALA is buggering for the U.S.A. and doesn't look normal. Both are obliged to acknowledge the cops with shiteaters. This doesn't go down well and gets a siren in response.

> SALA
>
> Make a left, make a left.

KEMP

What left? There is no left.

SALA

Any left.

*Any left takes them into a narrow
dead-end with an Everest of steps
the only way out. It's a no choice
and they can't stop anyway so down
they go. Pedestrians and washing
lines and expressions of sheer
horror as they descend like tandem
pilots in a wingless plane. Wipe out
a cartload of melons and more horror
at more stairs. SALA is still
buggering as six flights down they
vanish through somebody's front door.*

54 INT. SANDERSON'S OFFICE/CONFERENCE
ROOM. HIGH/RISE. DAY.

*Fourteen floors up and panoramic
views are incredible. Blue sea and
waterfront all the way from here to
the Hilton Hotel.*

*A pale glass partition separates
office reception from the conference
room (and I'm not sure which side
of the glass we'll be). But KEMP*

appears someplace looking consider-
ably refurbished — showered, shaved,
and a borrowed jacket and tie.
Although he's obviously late
SANDERSON puts out nice.

> KEMP
>
> Sorry, there were unexpected
> developments. I had to go
> home, start the day again.

> SANDERSON
>
> Tell me about it. Some days
> are two sizes too small.

By now they're in the conference
room. Greetings are at the end of a
white granite table, where ashtrays
and coffee cups tell the story.
SANDERSON lines it up to make
introductions.

> SANDERSON
>
> I'm afraid one or two of us
> had to leave. Mr Zimburger,
> you know, and this is Mr
> Green, of First National
> Maritime Bank.

Handshake with a man who only needs
fangs to be a full-blown snake. As

they sit SANDERSON checks out an empty coffee pot.

You want some coffee?

                    SEGURRA
I think we should move right
along, Hal. I gotta go.

                    SANDERSON
Sure.

*Various maps and architectural draw-
ings are scattered. SANDERSON
reaches for a leather album and
passes it to KEMP. It features
aerial photographs of an idyllic-
looking archipelago.*

                    SEGURRA
The island is owned by the
U.S. government, part of it
presently used as a target
range by the navy.
          (points it out)
We know from internal sources . . .

                    ZIMBURGER
          (chuckling)
Is that what you call me?

SEGURRA

We know that the government
are preparing to relinquish
the lease, and this place
wakes up as thirty-two square
miles of magnificent and
untouched real estate . .

SANDERSON

It'll knock your eyes out. No
prettier beaches in the
Caribbean.

ZIMBURGER

. . . orientated around one hell
of a beautiful marina . . .

KEMP

I thought it was one hotel?

SEGURRA

We start with one hotel.

SANDERSON

It's a foot in the door. Once
we are up and running, we are
servants of a market.

KEMP

Like here?

SANDERSON

Like here.

ZIMBURGER

You look worried, Mr Kemp?

SANDERSON

He's not worried. Paul and I
shared a tricky little night.
        (winks)
Right, Paul?
        (owns him)
Neither of us got much sleep.

At least one of them didn't. The
other one woke up grinning.

SEGURRA
        (to GREEN)
Gotta go.

MR GREEN

We'll leave you gentlemen to
it.

Everyone on their feet and escorted
by SANDERSON to the door.

MR GREEN

Has Mr Kemp signed the
papers?

SANDERSON
We're gonna do that right now.

KEMP
What am I actually signing?

SANDERSON
It's just a confidentiality
agreement, affirmation of
trust . . .

ZIMBURGER
. . . so we're sitting in
the same jacuzzi, if a turd
floats up . . .
        (smiles bad teeth)
if you know what I mean?

Handshakes and they're gone.
SANDERSON snatches a file from the
conference table and pilots KEMP to
the end of the room. There are a
couple of armchairs here and maybe a
desk. Gesturing a chair SANDERSON
finds the documents he's looking
for.

SANDERSON
Here you go. It's just a
technicality, Paul, means you
promise not to talk to anyone

about the project. How's the
head?

                    KEMP
Unpleasant.
          (signing)
Got to thank you again for
putting up the bail.

                  SANDERSON
I didn't put up anything,
it's held on my cognisance,
and I think it more than
likely to slip various minds.
This place is a sea of money,
Paul, unbelievable money,
practically every major corpor-
ation hides its cash off-
shore, and that's good news
for us, because we are the
shore . . . and not one
dollar that wings its way
into Puerto Rico pays a cent
in tax.

                    KEMP
Nothing?

                  SANDERSON
Not penny one. And that
includes chemical companies,

oil companies and mining
companies.
          (finds cigar)
There are twelve billion
dollars' worth of copper in
mountains less that twenty
miles from here.
          (cuts it)
A dozen billion dollars.
And then there's people like
me who know how to get it
out.
          (lights it)
So, putting it into context,
I don't envisage the breaking
of bones to get at a thousand
bucks.

*Anointing himself in smoke SANDERSON
finds another paper.*

Because you weren't here, I
agreed to an itinerary with
Zimburger on your behalf.
          (tossing it)
You'll be travelling down in
the morning, hope that's OK.

                    KEMP
What about the paper?

SANDERSON
I wouldn't worry too much
about the paper.
       (kind of weird)
It'll take care of itself . . .

*Time to stand and both do, KEMP
with something on his mind.*

What d'you need, Paul?

KEMP
Just in context of this
Zimburger thing, you think
there's a chance of an
advance? I don't like to ask
but Lotterman's pretty erratic
with the pay cheque. I need
to get hold of a car.

SANDERSON
You don't have a car?

KEMP
Nothing too reliable.
       (moreover)
And sooner or later, I'm going
to have to find a flat . . .

SANDERSON
We can help you with that,
when you get back, we'll sort
you out something with a view.
(picks up phone)
Carol, what do we have in the
garage? No, no, no, not that
OK. Sure yeah, that'll do just
fine.
(cans it)
Got a car for you, she'll
give you keys on the way out.

*Meantime he pulls a roll of dollars,
peels KEMP a tidy wad.*

Feels like five hundred.

*Nothing if he isn't generous. He
detains KEMP at the door.*

Oh, Paul, how's your afternoon?

KEMP
A half-written horoscope . . .

SANDERSON
Do me a favour, will you,
drive out to the beach and
pick up Chenault. I need her
downstairs by six.

— 150 —

55 EXT. HIGH/RISE BUILDING. BEACH/
SIDE. DAY.

*Fledgling palms at base of the
tower and entrance to underground
parking at the side of it.
Headlights and sound of a powerful
engine. The big V/8 pushes a Chevy
Corvette up the ramp with KEMP at
the wheel. It's blood red with wire
wheels and a poor boy's dream.
Suddenly the day got three hundred
and fifty horse power better.
Pausing in sunlight, KEMP takes off
ocean-side, like the cat that got
the cream.*

56 EXT. OCEAN BOULEVARD. JUNGLE ROAD.
DAY.

*No point in bullshitting the azure
sea stuff [and can we afford a
helicopter]. The Chevy is on its
way from Sanderson's office to
Sanderson's house. A variety of
shots do the job in whatever the
order. But it's a bit of an ODE
TO JOY, and I don't know whether
the band plays Beethoven or rock and
roll.*

57 INT. LIVING ROOM/TERRACE. BEACH
HOUSE. DAY.

*Black sequins, brown thighs, and a
flash of lace panties as CHENAULT
twirls a new outfit in front of
KEMP. He attempts objectivity when
all he wants is to rip it off and
fuck her dead. Grabbing another
creation she holds it up to herself.*

                    CHENAULT
  This one or the other one?

*Any one of them if she's in it.
They come with snazzy hats.*

                    KEMP
  What is it, a party?

                    CHENAULT
  It's for the carnival? Didn't
  he say anything about it?
          (he didn't)
  You've gotta come. We're all
  going down on the boat.

                    KEMP
  He didn't invite me.

CHENAULT
It isn't his carnival.
(posing)
OK, which dress, this one, or
the other one?

KEMP
I think I like the other one.

58 INT. CHEVY CONVERTIBLE/COUNTRY ROADS.
DAY.

*Somebody else's car and somebody
else's lady but apart from that the
afternoon couldn't be more perfect.
All legs and lipstick CHENAULT
radiates sex from the passenger
seat. It is an unequivocal reality,
like the big V/8 throbbing under
KEMP's foot. Power plus her pouting
equals an intoxication.*

KEMP
Love this car.

CHENAULT
Did he give it to you?

KEMP
I wish. It's fast . . .

*Everything she does is like some-
thing to do with sex. What she just
did was press in the cigar-lighter
and use it on a pair of cigarettes.
Puts one in his mouth and he tastes
the lipstick. He looks across and
gets heat from the same lips.*

                    CHENAULT
          You want a little bet?

                    KEMP
          A bet about what?

                    CHENAULT
          That you scream before I do?

                    KEMP
          I scream before you do?
                    (smiling)
          In relation to what?

                    CHENAULT
          How fast does it go?

                    KEMP
          I don't know . . .

                    CHENAULT
          That's the bet.

He enjoys the flirting but isn't too fascinated by the idea.

> KEMP
> I already crashed one car
> today.

> CHENAULT
> OK. I'll go sit in the foyer
> and wait for him.

She's just doing what she does and KEMP is a willing victim.

> KEMP
> What do I get if I win?

> CHENAULT
> I'll let you know if you do.

Which for all the world sounds like something involving his dick. A freeway sign happens to offer itself and KEMP goes for it. I'm not into describing what the rush does to CHENAULT, but she's loving it, and so is he. 90/100/110 on the clock and the Chevy hasn't finished yet. Clouds of ominous dust begin to mass in its wake and here's why. This end of the road is still under

*construction, intermittent placards
urging caution. A hundred and thirty
miles an hour and still some more
to go. CHENAULT's breasts are
pressed against her shirt in a fabu-
lous description. 'Faster, Faster,'
as Mr Thompson once put it, 'until
the thrill of speed overcomes the
fear of death.'*

*Flirting with CHENAULT is different
to flirting with death. Out of road
and the tyres are burning. Parallel
streaks of rubber put down by the
brakes. The Chevy ploughs through a
bunch of wood chevrons and totals
a sign advertising a skull and
cross bones. It stops at death's
door. Paralysed with terror and
exhilaration, they stare without
questioning who will yell first,
spontaneously both scream at the
same time.*

*An echo sounds over a tropical
valley and they're literally yards
from a precipice. When construction
continues it will feature a bridge
across a gorge. Meanwhile it's a
three-hundred-foot drop. They have
reached a dead end and a sign*

*actually says so. It isn't clear
whether the symbolism of this
statement registers for KEMP.
Quitting the Chevy both stare across
an unspoiled landscape, a beautiful
vista of sunlight and mist.*

> CHENAULT
> You will come to St Thomas,
> won't you?

*Something entirely different has
overtaken CHENAULT in her eyes.
There's a kiss coming up and neither
can prevent it.*

> KEMP
> *(after kiss)*
> Why'd you do that?

> CHENAULT
> Didn't you want me to?

*He's got the car, got the girl, but
it's a road to nowhere.*

> KEMP
> C'mon, I'll take you back.

They walk towards the car and into a slow dissolve. Piano music seeps in, daft but appropriate, 'These Foolish Things'.

59 INT/EXT. TERRACE. AL'S BAR. DUSK.

I forget the name of the pianist, but he's playing as usual to people who don't hear. Al's is relatively busy, several recognisable JOURNALISTS who's names we don't know. MOBURG is busy with rum and KEMP at a nearby table with a full ashtray and bottle of Coke. Running a hand through hair KEMP stubs it. Simultaneously SALA appears. Bandaged and furtive he joins his companions.

                    KEMP
    Where have you been?

                    SALA
      Asleep.

Ordering rum he slaps a newspaper on the table. It's called El Diario *and headlines a picture of SALA and KEMP arriving at the police station. The text is in Spanish but clear enough.*

KEMP
Where'd they get this?

SALA
I don't remember.
(freaked)
I've been slightly avoiding
Lotterman.

MOBURG
You got me to thank for your
freedom.

SALA
Thanks.
(dying)
I have a feeling of total
anxiety trying to put my
anxieties together in a
single, coherent lump.

MOBURG
Report it stolen.

KEMP
I told him about the car.

SALA
They *saw us* driving it.
(rum arrives)
I'm fucked without a car.

> KEMP

I got us a car.

> MOBURG
> (sneering)

It's the Chevy outside,
belongs to Mr Sanderson.

> KEMP

So what?
> (standing)

I gotta type this up.

Rum in one, SALA goes with him,
with wise words from MOBURG.

> MOBURG

Those who stoop to kiss ass,
are already in position to
get shat on.

60 INT. NEWSROOM. THE DAILY STAR.
NIGHT.

*Three hours to print and the dynamic
is evident. Chatter of typewriters
telex and faces on phones. There's a
lot of row, but most of it coming
from behind LOTTERMAN's office
windows.*

*A full-blown shout-out appears to be
in progress, and if you can avoid
it you will. SALA and KEMP cross
the newsroom trying for just that.
Bump into WOLSLEY on his way to his
desk.*

WOLSLEY

I don't know what's going on
. . . he's freaking out and
we're down twelve pages.

*It's a sour atmosphere indeed.
LOTTERMAN's door suddenly flies open
and MORRELL comes out shouting. He's
had it with LOTTERMAN, had it with
this pathetic little paper, and quits.*

LOTTERMAN

You better frigging do it
. . . I see your filthy
animal face again, I'll have
you locked up.

*Wig askance he glares after him,
switches attention to SALA.*

And what particular part of
the building are you creeping
towards, Sala?

> SALA

Darkroom.

> LOTTERMAN

Cops are looking for you.

> SALA

Looking for me?

> LOTTERMAN

Looking for you.

*On retreat to his office he snatches
a nearby El Diario.*

And it ain't just that.

*Tossing the paper in the air he
bulldozers behind a slammed door.
SALA pushes on to the darkroom with
KEMP in his wake.*

61 INT. DARKROOM. THE DAILY STAR.
    NIGHT.

*A dangling wire activates a red
light. SALA crumples into one of
the benches, rousing himself only to
find his stash.*

                    SALA
What a day . . . what a week . . .
        (pouring)
I tell you, I'm outta here,
one way to frigging Mexico.

*He offers a swig of rum, but KEMP
declines.*

                    KEMP
I've given up. Listen, I got
a trip tomorrow, Sanderson's
island.

                    SALA
Oh dear.

                    KEMP
It's green money . . . and
I'm thinking of cutting across
for the carnival? They got a
carnival in St Thomas?

                    SALA
I know. Fun.

                    KEMP
Why don't you come with me?
Give the cops a few days to
forget it.

62 EXT. BIG SEA/BIG SKY. DAY.

*Wide and low above cobalt-coloured
ocean. A seaplane enters frame, flat
out towards a horizon of tropical
islands.*

63 INT. PASSENGER CABIN. SEAPLANE. DAY.

*Six seats available with ZIMBURGER
and a weaselish-looking associate
called MONK occupying the middle
row. Behind them are KEMP and
SALA. The grown-ups study documents,
a* New York Times *emerging from one
of the briefcases. It's loud in
here and ZIMBURGER has to shout
as he shoves the paper over a
shoulder.*

> ZIMBURGER
> You see this?
> *(news feature)*
> Your Russian buddies.

> KEMP
> They're not personal friends.

> ZIMBURGER
> They're in your paper.

>   SALA
>   *(reading)*
> This is about India?

>   ZIMBURGER
> Same thing. Commies. If the
> British had any balls they'd
> take it back. We got a
> twenty-four-hundred-megaton
> missile-gap. That is a short-
> fall of two bilion, four
> hundred million tons of
> T.N.T. equivalent.

SALA mouths, 'He's a nut,' but KEMP enjoys the bullshitting.

>   KEMP
> Those are frightening figures,
> Major.

>   ZIMBURGER
> Damn A, they're frightening,
> and if Kennedy gets in,
> they're frightening yet . . .
>   *(grabbing the paper)*
> . . . that prick in the
> Kremlin wants to do it, but
> he doesn't dare . . . by
> definition, the communist mind
> is that of a coward . . .

SALA
What d'you mean, a yellow red?

ZIMBURGER
I mean two hundred and fifty-
six Polaris submarines.

*The airplane banks revealing an
atoll of picture postcards.*

We need to take action before
1962 or, mark my words, the
entire western hemisphere will
be a smoking ruin.

KEMP
Or covered in hotels.

ZIMBURGER
How's that?

SALA
He said, he couldn't agree
with you more.

64 EXT. TROPICAL ISLAND. DAY.

*The seaplane touches down and taxis
to reveal a tropical paradise. If
there's any place on earth that
should be protected from humans, this*

is it. The aircraft parks on the shoreline and the humans get out.

At a moment convenient to him ZIMBURGER puts a whisper to KEMP in respect to SALA and his cameras.

> ZIMBURGER
> Who'd you say he was?

> KEMP
> He's my consultant.

As they arrive on virgin sand there's a sinister, atmospheric whistle, followed by a distant thud of high-explosive. You wouldn't know what it was without ZIMBURGER who's proud to explain.

> ZIMBURGER
> Our guys . . . twelve inch naval, fourteen miles out.

65 EXT. HEADLAND/BEACH. ISLAND. DAY.

ZIMBURGER leads a way down through palms. Making their way across clinically white sand they approach a stand of tents. In near proximity are blackened remains of a burned-out hut.

*The tents are actually make-shift
offices, open at the front with
awnings against the sun. Cheap
aluminium furniture and everyone in
shades. On arrival ZIMBURGER selects
one of the faces to introduce. A
regular looking chap in his early
thirties.*

>   ZIMBURGER
>   Mr Lazar, our much put-upon
>   site-architect. Mr Monk, I
>   think you know?

>   MONK/WEASEL
>   I assist Mr Green, First
>   Maritime Bank.

>   ZIMBURGER
>   This is Mr Kemp, of the *New
>   York Times* . . . and what do
>   you say your name was?
>   *(SALA says it)*
>   Mr Sala, of the American
>   Travel Writers' Association.

*Handshakes over and apologies for
the clutter. Clearing a table
ZIMBURGER finds space to snap locks
on his briefcase.*

ZIMBURGER
Mr Kemp is preparing our
brochure, 'Wish you were here'.

LAZAR
Beer in the cooler, gentlemen.
(gesturing)
I have everything next door.

ZIMBURGER
What happened to the huts?

LAZAR
Burned down last week, hence
the new home.

MONK
We had warning of this, we're
gonna need security.

ZIMBURGER
Razor wire. Six hundred yards
out.

Chatter from walkie-talkies, plus
thud of distant explosions.

LAZAR
Where do you wanna start, Mr
Kemp?

                    KEMP
     I think with a walk.

66 EXT. PARADISE BEACH. DAY

     KEMP and SALA stroll the waterline
     about a hundred yards from the
     tents. Anywhere you want it is
     beauty and SALA takes photographs.
     KEMP fixes a different set of
     pictures in his head.

                    KEMP
       Ten thousand waiters, maids,
       bellhops, janitors and
       clerks. Plus whores for the
       fat man.

     A voice hollers from the tents.
     ZIMBURGER wants them back.

                    SALA
       Hard to believe they'd do it?

                    KEMP
       You know what I'd like to do,
       murder the lot of them, leave
       them for the crabs.

67 INT/EXT. AWNING [SECOND TENT].
    BEACH. DAY.

*An architectural model of the envis-
aged development is focus of discussions. Contours of the hills are set
out with various lozenges of balsa-
wood, painted blue or red.*

*Dozens of tiny boats are glued in
the 'marina', overshadowed by a pair
of high-rise hotels. The rest of the
facsimile is cluttered with villas,
like someone won everything on a
Monopoly board.*

              ZIMBURGER
           (all but drooling)
    . . . this and this are the
    main hotels, twenty-two
    floors, guardians of the bay,
    so to speak . . .

              KEMP
    Why the different colours?

              MONK
    Blue for public dissemination,
    red for the investors.

                    ZIMBURGER
. . . hill villas, ocean
condos,
          (pointing out)
Marina, parking for two
thousand cars . . .

                    SALA
There's no roads?

                    ZIMBURGER
          (joshing)
Damn it, Lazar! You forgot
roads! We're building them.

                    MONK
Where we came in will ulti-
mately become a roll-on ferry
port.

                    KEMP
You think cars are a good
idea?

                    MONK
          (misreading KEMP)
We have some very healthy
projections. The auto popula-
tion in Puerto Rico is
growing at twice the speed of
the indigenous birth rate —

for every kid that's born, we
got two cars.

                    LAZAR
Plus, auto-rental.

                 ZIMBURGER
It's a valuable franchise.
Let's have some lunch . . .

68 EXT. PARADISE BEACH. DAY.

*Pink and gold masses on the horizon,
not actually sunset but on its way.
KEMP has hauled one of the
aluminium chairs to the shoreline,
sits alone with bare feet in the
sea, indulging some sombre mood. He
reads [V.O.] from a grubby paperback.*

'And I had done a hellish
thing,
And it would work 'em woe:
For all averred, I had killed
the bird
That made the breeze to blow . . .
Ah wretch! said they, the
bird to slay,
That made the breeze to
blow!'

Big thoughts occupy KEMP. SALA arrives with a can of beer.

> SALA
>
> Talking to that architect kinda guy. He's going to St Thomas, if you want a ride?

> KEMP
>
> When?

> SALA
>
> How do I know when?
> *(drinks)*
> When he's finished here?

The silence belongs to KEMP. A while before he disturbs it.

> KEMP
>
> You know what Oscar Wilde said: 'they know the price of everything, and the value of nothing'.

69 EXT. PLAZA. OLD TOWN. SAINT THOMAS. DAY.

Carnival comes down like an explosion. Trumpets on the cut and the rest is colour and sunshine. So many

*people in the plaza you can barely
move, just go with the rhythm of
pounding steel drums. Most of the
faces are black, but white Americans
here and there in carnival hats.
Everyone's in hats and feathers and
crazy paint, and everyone's swilling
booze.*

*Rum and music are everywhere,
conspiring to push the energy. Every
sidewalk has its make-shift booze
stall where violent slugs are doled
out in paper cups. I don't know
where KEMP and SALA turned up, but
suddenly they're in the thick if it.*

*A shot of rum costs twenty-five
cents, and BARMEN work feverishly to
supply demand. KEMP pushes through
and finally gets served.*

                    KEMP
  Two rums, two cups of ice.

                    SALA
  I thought you'd given up?

                    KEMP
  I finally beat my will power.

Happy grins as they hit them in one. Shift themselves as a truck hoots through. Another steel band on the back of it, with some juicy-looking dancing girls dressed as pineapples.

Maybe an hour later. Maybe only minutes. KEMP and SALA are the other side of the plaza dancing in a throng of people. You might call it dancing. But in fact it's a human snake shunting through the crowd in synchronised jive to the Salsa Band.

Being drunk is the only requirement to join in and KEMP and SALA are fully qualified. By the time they find a way out, both are dripping with sweat and more booze is the antidote.

SALA fixes it at the nearest stall. KEMP points to a colonial-looking building across the square. It's a sizable hotel and he wants a detour to change his shirt, get a wash-up.

70   INT. GROUND FLOOR. COLONIAL HOTEL. DAY.

A slightly more up-market throng,

*although almost as packed as the
street. Lazy ceiling fans and
calypso Music upstairs.*

*Considerably freshened [clean shirt,
clean teeth and shaved] KEMP emerges
from the subterranean stairs [dirty
laundry confined to his rucksack].
He looks about for SALA, and gets
the eye from various quarters. A lot
of talent in respect of ladies, and
if you cared to you could fuck
yourself billious. Following the
music he pushes up a staircase
towards another bar.*

71 INT. UPSTAIRS BAR/BALCONY. HOTEL.
DAY.

*Just as loud in here but less
people. It doesn't take long to find
SALA. He's propping the bar with a
COUPLE OF GIRLS, one with a guitar
slung across her back. Introductions
are made but KEMP doesn't really
hear. 'Rosy is a singer.' No beauty,
but better than a kick in the
balls. KEMP gets rum instead of a
handshake and makes his way towards
the balcony. From here you can see
right across the square. It's an*

anarchy of madness and colour and
you'd have to be real lucky to
single anyone out. KEMP just got
lucky. Can it really be her? She
vanishes momentarily behind a
phalanx of faces, arms waving
above her head as she sways with
the music. He waits, and stares,
and she turns. It's definitely
CHENAULT.

72 EXT. PLAZA. DAY.

KEMP shoves his way through the
insanity, SALA behind holding ROSY's
hand. They can't find CHENAULT and
SALA doesn't care. Yakking in
Spanish he's persuaded to escort his
date to a dance hall. A rendezvous
is agreed and KEMP pushes on.

One of the coolest spots to dance
is under the fountain. A breeze puts
haze in the air. And there she is,
shirt stuck to her breasts and focus
of much attention as she flaunts it
for the local boys. All want to
dance real close, and many do. But
then she sees KEMP, embracing him
like a lost love.

> KEMP

Where's Hal?

> CHENAULT

Boat . . .
>   *(taking his hand)*
C'mon . . . we gotta find my
girlfriend.

*Half drunk and totally happy, he's
pleased to get led away.*

73 EXT. STONE STAIRWAY. OLD TOWN/
HARBOUR. DAY.

*Ancient steps find a way through
crooked houses. CHENAULT leads
descent towards the port. Apart from
the white SOUTH AFRICAN GIRL, all
are more or less drunk. KEMP may
already have misgivings, but SALA
and ROSY [plus guitar] are too
involved to notice. The stairs
finally arrive at a quayside.*

*Anybody who's been to St Tropez will
get the picture. This is where the
money docks. Sloops and up-market
yachts from Miami and Bermuda sport
French, British and American flags.
The rich are showing off their*

wealth and CHENAULT seems familiar with not a few. Waves to various faces taking sun and champagne on their decks. Meanwhile an alfresco restaurant is being set up on the quay to feed the maritime bourgeoisie.

KEMP
Is this a good idea?

CHENAULT
He's in happy mode.

74 EXT. SANDERSON'S YACHT. HARBOUR.
DAY.

Like walking the plank in reverse they invade a small drinks party. If SANDERSON was in happy mode it may just have changed. But ever the diplomat he keeps it to himself. Several recognisable faces among the introductions. SEGURRA with his pretty lady, and CHENAULT who doesn't understand the atmospheric and pours her new pals champagne. SANDERSON, however, escorts KEMP to the bows for a discreet word or two.

SANDERSON
Did you take Sala to the
island?
          (no answer)
You shouldn't have done that,
Paul, it's why we have a
confidentiality agreement?

KEMP
He isn't interested.

SANDERSON
He's got a mouth like an A.P.
wire . . . I don't know what
he was doing there, and sure
as shit, don't know what he's
doing here?

*Or in other words, what's KEMP
doing here? Before they can get into
it there is an interruption. Brash
tooting announces the arrival of an
open ex-military jeep decorated with
garlands of flowers. It's driven by
a fifty-year-old piss-artist with a
racy young thing at his side. More
money than brains, he stands in his
seat to wave roses and champagne.
Clearly they are friends SANDERSON
expected.*

SANDERSON
Hey, Digby . . . My man.

KEMP
If you want us to leave?

DIGBY and his sexy little lady are already on the gangplank.

SANDERSON
(*loaded*)
Be my guest.

75 EXT. SANDERSON'S YACHT. DUSK.

ROSY plays her guitar, a sad song of the people, and she's actually very good. Dead champagne bottles upended in the ice-buckets, a lot of booze gone down. Sun going down too, at end of the day and beginning of the evening. SANDERSON and some of his guests are apparently below taking a siesta.

The pretty SOUTH AFRICAN GIRL, DIGBY and his LADY are still on deck, plus CHENAULT and KEMP. He's in love with her and she's unobtainable. With ROSY still singing he gets up and drifts to the bow of the boat. SALA is crashed on the deck in inebriated sleep. KEMP stares across reflections of the harbour, watching the onslaught of another enormous sunset.

He doesn't need to look back to know CHENAULT is looking at him. But you need better cards for that kind of game. ROSY finishes her ballad and now you can hear music from the bars. The waterfront is waking, mysterious hotels with red and yellow lights, and people heading for parties aboard the yachts.

CHENAULT

Not going glum on us, are you?

A sensual touch of fingertips, he had no idea she was there.

KEMP

Just thoughts.

> CHENAULT
> What's the book?

> KEMP
> *Rime of the Ancient Mariner.*
> Written in 1797, by a junkie
> called Coleridge. Wrote it
> when he was twenty-five
> years old. I been dragging
> a typewriter around with
> me for ten, and written
> nothing.

> CHENAULT
> You've written some books.

> KEMP
> I got no voice. I don't know
> how to write like me.

76 INT. ALFRESCO RESTAURANT. QUAYSIDE.
NIGHT.

*The obscenely rich dine on their
schooners, the filthy rich dine
here. The glitterati scoff their way
through suckling pigs and Cristal
under crucibles of flame and fairy-
lights. They're almost done at
SEGURRA's table when KEMP pitches up.*

— 184 —

KEMP
Thanks for the afternoon,
maybe see you in town . . .

CHENAULT
Where are you going?

She's got the new dress on. Looks
too delicious to look at. KEMP
gestures over to SALA/ROSY, waiting
at the peripheries.

KEMP
Her brother's playing in a
band . . . we're gonna go
check it out . . .

CHENAULT
We wanna come.

SANDERSON
I'll rephrase that, we don't
wanna come.

CHENAULT
Yes we do, us girls wanna
dance.

SANDERSON
You're dancing tomorrow.

CHENAULT
What's with the coming to a
carnival if everything is
pre-planned? I want to dance
tonight, and if you won't
take me, I'll go with them.

DIGBY
She's got you trumped, Hal.

SANDERSON
Sit down. You're drunk.

CHENAULT
So what? So's everyone else.

*SANDERSON could cut KEMP's throat,
DIGBY defuses the moment.*

DIGBY
Oh, come on, let's do it
. . . it may be amusing.

77 EXT. BACK STREETS. ST THOMAS.
NIGHT.

*High above the port where tourists
would never go. Somewhere downtown
there's a firework display. DIGBY's
jeep finds a way through a narrow
street. He drives with SANDERSON*

and *CHENAULT* up front. His
GIRLFRIEND sits in the back with
SALA and *ROSY*. The *SNOOTY GIRL* is
drunk enough to perch on *KEMP's* lap.
Blue lights come into view together
with a throb of night-music.

78 INT. NIGHTCLUB. ST THOMAS. NIGHT.

A place where mother-fuckers congre-
gate. It's a hell-hole of sweat and
sex and *CHENAULT* can't wait to get
into it. A reggae band pound it out
with no exits. The ambiance is so
loud and so dynamic either you're a
part of it or you're in the street.
At some point it may be noticed
that *KEMP* and his gang are the only
white faces. But that isn't neces-
sarily important. At least not yet.
The band are at the end of their
set. Much rum and black faces in
blue light. Not entirely to
SANDERSON's taste. But everybody
happy to meet *ROSY'S BROTHER*, and he
gets preferential service at the
bar.

                    SALA
        You want rum or beer?

CHENAULT
Both.

*Everything in close-up because
there's no other way of seeing. You
can smell the dope even if you don't
know what it is. Even DIGBY is a
part of the energy, although
SANDERSON probably fakes it.
Whistles and claps as the line-up
changes. Star turn is a rather
different outfit. Thunder stabs from
an electric guitar. Two hundred
mouths yell encouragement as they
snap in the jacks, put out shocks of
feedback.*

*Once again I refer to HOUND DOG
TAYLOR. His is the kind of music I
want. A real friendly face with a
Strat and a grin hits a slug from
his on-stage bottle. 'You alright?'
'You alright?' Sure they're alright.
Two hundred faces alright.*

*Adrenalin out of a raw guitar.
Caribbean turned into black rock and
roll. Walls of black muscle put eyes
on the little white girls. CHENAULT
and her GIRLFRIEND are riding cloud
nine.*

'Kitchen Sink Boogie', or something
similar. Rock like it's coming out of
the floor. The whole room is busted
but SANDERSON becomes an observer.
Look at this guy, dancing behind his
girl with hands inside her blouse.
Black Angel with red lipstick. Almost
fucking her. It's all over for DIGBY
and he drags his sweltering LADY
out. Has to shout to get heard. OK,
they're leaving. SANDERSON is
leaving. CHENAULT isn't.

> SANDERSON
> We're going, Chenault . . .

He grabs her wrist but she isn't
having it. Just the beginning of
something tense. If he wants to go,
that's OK, but she wants to dance.
A whole bunch of blue-black faces
dance around her. Her fuses are
blown and SANDERSON moves on KEMP.
He brought her here. He better get
her out. KEMP will try.

> HOUND DOG
> . . . I just wanna get funky
> with you

*Dirty fucking music. CHENAULT in
there somewhere. A white girl-magnet,
black hands clapping, twisting in
her spangled skirt. Pretty legs
and bitch guitar. 'You alright?'
'You alright?' You don't know
where else to look because nothing
is happening but HOUND DOG and
CHENAULT strutting her stuff.*

*They rhythm is repetitive.
Insistent. Hear it once and you
understand what's developing.
CHENAULT is becoming more provoca-
tive and outrageous and people are
making space for her.*

*A variety of partners evolve into
one. He's a powerful-looking BLACK
STUD sleek with muscle. Dancing
close to CHENAULT she mirrors his
sexuality like it's some kind of
competition.*

*'Do it like that.' Clapping hands
encourage the excitement. CHENAULT
hardly needs it. Promiscuity like a
narcotic. She seems as mesmerised by
the music as by the man. It's a
difficult arena to invade and when*

KEMP attempts it the response is predictable.

He shouts to get heard but it's just another voice. He tries to grab her but gets grabbed himself.

> HOUND DOG
> . . . she's dancin', man . .
> Incidentally, this is my
> finger in your face . . .

It points him backwards. Like how about the exit? By now a sweltering wall has formed around the dancers. CHENAULT and her PARTNER are the only show in town. She's advertising and he wants it. Unbuttons his shirt and hauls it off, and now it's her turn. Wild applause as she opens her top.

Beautiful breasts in a chic silk brassiere. It's a hard-on for everyone but SANDERSON. This is every man's bad dream. The greater her sensuality, the greater the rage, and greater the promise of violence. He shouts but she doesn't hear. CHENAULT has completely lost the plot. Arms above her head, she puts out while her paramour raises the hem of her dress.

Do it like that. Do it like
that.

*She's doing it like they want it
and they clamber tables for a better
view. Her exquisite dress becomes a
lascivious experiment. She teases
him to raise it higher, and soon
there is nothing between her high
heels and panties but legs. He lifts
the dress right over her head and
the music wants more. Everyone wants
more, wants her naked, maybe she
wants it too.*

*There may be worse places to get
into a fight but it's hard to
imagine one. The dynamic is so over-
wound it's going to snap and when
it does SANDERSON tastes blood.
Blood all over his white silk suit.
You don't want to get hit by this
guy twice and count yourself lucky
to be leaving here alive.*

*Venomous eyes and supremely bad
vibes. The dilemma belongs to KEMP.
He's got to get SANDERSON out before
he kills someone (or more likely)
someone kills him. But more than
that, he's got to extract CHENAULT*

*without getting killed himself.
Midway through the crowd SANDERSON
re-freaks. He lashes out and hands
that try to restrain him rip shit
out of his suit. He's going crazy.
One welcome face emerges from
fracas. SALA is among many who
struggle to get SANDERSON out. KEMP
pushes back into a nightmare. And if
anything it got worse.*

*You might just see the blade, just a
flash in flashing light. It comes
out of the frenzy, deftly severing
the back of CHENAULT's bra. Straps
slip off her shoulders, for a moment
she clasps it to her breasts. Brute
carnality that no one could stop.
Not her. Not anybody. And that means
you, white man.*

*The vibes couldn't be more
dangerous. Last thing KEMP sees is
the brassiere held in the air, then
kissed by her partner.*

79 INT/EXT. ENTRANCE/STREET. NIGHTCLUB.
NIGHT.

*Some bad stuff has gone down on the
steps. SANDERSON crouches at the*

bottom like a crushed snail. Clearly grief with the brothers ended bad. One of the sleeves hangs off his suit, and the rest is dirt and blood. SALA says, 'They called a cab.' Any attempt to get him on his feet is aggressively rejected, SANDERSON wants no help from KEMP. Here comes the cab, and somehow he gets bundled in and somebody slams the door.

Music from the club is drowned in a roar. Maybe they're already fucking her? Tail lights vanish down the hill. Pandemonium inside and KEMP climbs steps to confront it. But I don't think so, and neither do the faces at the top of the stairs. He gets jive from the MAN IN THE HAT, and this place is closed.

KEMP
I gotta get the girl.

MAN IN HAT
She having a good time.
(you deaf?)
I said, we closed, man.

Bad eyes in a harsh face and what he means SALA understands.

— 194 —

SALA
No way, Paul. No way.

80 EXT. BEACH. ST THOMAS. DAWN.

*Wide over the beach with thunder in
the air. Gold in black cloud. It
won't rain now. But it's going to
rain tomorrow. KEMP pitches up in
dispirited mood, it's two parts
hangover and the rest anxiety for
CHENAULT. SALA is sprawled on
cameras (at least one of them got
some sleep). KEMP sits next to him
and tells the story just as soon as
he wakes to hear.*

KEMP
I looked everywhere, man, even
went to the gendarme.

SALA
And . . .

KEMP
We went up there . . .
nothing . . . nobody there,
just an old woman with a mop
. . . and she's more help
than the cop . . .

— 195 —

> (mimicking)
> . . . 'What can I do if your
> girlfriend likes someone
> else?' etcetera, etcetera.

*A conclusion SALA agrees with, but
first he finishes a yawn.*

                    SALA
He's right about that, Paul,
she's not your girlfriend . . .
Did you sleep?

                    KEMP
I don't remember.

                    SALA
We're gonna need some breakfast, then we'll think it
through . . .
          (lacing boots)
Maybe she went back to the
boat? Did you try the boat?

                    KEMP
I don't think he'd let her on.

81 EXT. HARBOUR. OLD TOWN. DAY.

*More thunder and sky like lead, like
the entire harbour is sleeping it*

*off. Chairs and tables stacked at
last night's restaurant. Here and
there staff are beginning to clear
up, decks washed on one or two
yachts. SALA munches a hamburger. He
and KEMP approach SANDERSON's berth
with understandable feelings of
unease. They expect the worst, and
get it.*

*Only one craft in the harbour is on
the move and it is SANDERSON's.
Exhaust gurgles from the stern as he
backs it out. SANDERSON sees KEMP
as he sees him.*

KEMP
Is she with you?

*No answer from SANDERSON, a dozen
feet of water between them.*

Is she with you?

*SANDERSON slams a lever across,
propellers change direction.*

SANDERSON
Why don't you mind your own
god-damned business?

*Thrusting a hand out he snaps
fingers like KEMP is a waiter.*

I want the keys? The Chevy?

*Keys are found and tossed across,
expertly caught on arrival.*

You blew it, Kemp . . .

*He shoves forward on the lever, the
yacht heads for open sea.*

82 EXT. STREET. OLD SAN JUAN. DAY.

*Music survives the dissolve into a
rain-swept street. KEMP shelters
under a battered black umbrella. He
and SALA inspect a clapped-out motor-
bike and sidecar. Owned by MOBURG,
it's evidently for sale. KEMP circles
it isolating deficiencies.*

KEMP
I've seen better tyres hanging
over the side of a tug.

MOBURG
You want it or not?

KEMP looks at SALA [beggars and choosers]. Yeah they want it.

83 INT. STAIRWAY/APARTMENT. OLD
    BUILDING. DAY.

MOBURG wheezes up the stairs in his saturated raincoat. He carries a tool bag full of spares [which include a busted wing-mirror] and KEMP brings up the rear with a spare wheel.

> MOBURG
>
> Everyone turns up for the Friday cheque, right . . . no cheque, no Lotterman. So I go round to see that unforgivably ugly wife of his, and she tells me, he's gone to Miami.

> SALA
>
> For what?

> MOBURG
>
> You don't know, I don't know, but the Scabs are back.

SALA unlocks and they shuffle in. Rain lashes the windows and a cock crows. KEMP carries his wheel into the kitchen.

                    MOBURG (COND)
        Since Morrell went, the *News*
        took a turn for the worse.

        Upending empties he looks for a
        bottle with something in it.

        Is anything in the spinner?

                    SALA
        We need a fresh sack.

        KEMP hacks rust off the wheel. And
        discovers nothing else.

                    MOBURG
        Maybe I could interest you
        gentleman in something else.

                    KEMP
        Like what
                (the wheel)
        death?

                    MOBURG
        Like the most powerful drug
        in the history of narcotics.

        A small brown bottle is produced
        from his pocket. It's got a rubber-

*bulb. The kind of thing they dish
out for earache.*

> MOBURG (COND)
> I'm not at liberty to
> disclose or discuss . . . all
> I can tell you is, this stuff
> is so powerful they give it
> to Communists.

> KEMP
> Who does?

> MOBURG
> The F.B.I.

> SALA
> Why would the F.B.I. get
> Communists high?

> MOBURG
> That, I can't help you with.
>   *(the breath zone)*
> You take it like eye-drops.

> SALA
> In the eye?

> MOBURG
> So I understand. It makes the

eye see things . . . you see
a different reality.

> KEMP
> *(examining vial)*
> What d'you want for it?

> MOBURG
> I'll throw it in with the
> bike, if you do me a favour?

> KEMP
> All right, what's the favour?

> MOBURG
> I want one of you to come
> into the bathroom with
> me?

*Looks like SALA's call and
KEMP heads to his room for
money.*

> KEMP
> Fifty dollars, right?

*Slam cut on the much depleted wad.
KEMP pulls fifty for the bike/drugs.
Walks back to the room where SALA
is disgusted.*

SALA

He wants me to look at his
dick. I flatly refused.

KEMP

What does he want you to look
at it for?

SALA

He says there's something
wrong with it.

MOBURG

It's a gentleman's matter.

SALA

I'm not looking at it.

MOBURG

OK. Give me the drugs back.

Anything but give the drugs back.
KEMP looks at MOBURG and then spots
his tool-bag. The busted wing-mirror
is prominent.

KEMP

OK. I'll look at it . . .
view it in the mirror.

Actors can do this better than I can write it. KEMP gets behind MOBURG and the lowered trouser. Tension in teeth as he brings the wing-mirror into play. It makes your mouth water.

MOBURG

Is it clap?

KEMP

A standing ovation.

84 INT. SALA'S APARTMENT. NIGHT.

Enormous close-up of an eye. Drip, Drip, Drip. The liquid goes in. They don't know the dose or even what the drug is. I can help them with that. It's called Lysergic Acid Diethylamide Tartrate. In a year or two it will be known as LSD.

Candlelight separates KEMP and SALA. They share a constant reciprocity of anticipation. Anyone familiar with LSD will know that fuck all happens until something actually happens. They are not familiar with LSD and don't know what it'll be or when. Thus they sit in a vacuum of deflated expectation.

                    KEMP
We'll give it another five
minutes.

                    SALA
And then what?

[P.O.V. TV] across the alleyway, they
watch I Love Lucy, via binoculars.
Because it's slashing with rain the
sound isn't so good. But SALA seems
amused by Miss Ball's jokes.

                    KEMP
How long since we took it?

                    SALA
I don't know . . . a while . . .

                    KEMP
It's bullshit, isn't it?

Bullshit or not, there's something
quite extraordinary about that rain
running down the window. It seems
extraordinary liquid and KEMP aban-
dons binoculars to look at it. A
weird illusion. It's just rivulets
of rain. But it's glistening rain.
Almost imperceptibly the room becomes
more closely observed. Everything

*requires a close-up. SALA opens a
beer, and the hiss around the cap is
as important as anything else.*

*KEMP lights a cigarette and that's
important too. The Zippo needs a
close-up to fully cover the event.
Fire escapes the flint like an F.16
taking off. Inhalation makes the end
of his cigarette very red. He tosses
the pack on the table and watches
it land. For some occult reason, it
seems to have a significance. He
stares at SALA, still nothing is
happening.*

                    KEMP
   You feel anything?

*KEMP blows smoke rings. Looks at
rain on the windows. Silver rain
trickles down and in its way is
curiously beautiful. He might wonder
why he'd never noticed that before.
[But it rarely rains so why should
he?] And anyway his attention has
switched to the GOLDFISH. Like
everything else it requires a close-
up and then [somewhat weirdly] it's
own point of view.*

[P.O.V. GOLDFISH.] It stares out via fish-eye lens from one world to another. Watches KEMP and SALA peering at each other in the yellow light. Maybe only the FISH can hear the Music? Without music this alchemy can't be happening. It's called, 'Col Lengo', by an American named RALPH TOWNER. His composition features nothing but a double bass and drum. It results in a sublime mix of expectation and menace. Similar sentiments attend KEMP and SALA. They've taken the most powerful substance on planet earth, and the bastard just cut in.

No way do I try to describe the mechanics of this sequence with a typewriter. Only a camera can tell the tale. Don't ask how, but both MUSIC and FISH-LENS have quit the bowl, and are out in the room. The fish-eye doesn't survive long, but the MUSIC intensifies and begins to own the environment.

This isn't going to be an entirely pleasant introduction to LSD. What you might call variable. They stare

*from opposite chairs. Everything
looks normal, but it isn't. A
cock crows [thrice] and the MUSIC
comes into its own. [It can't be
stressed enough that without this
sinister rhapsody nothing can be
envisaged.] The Double Bass is reso-
nant with malign promise. KEMP
knows something AWFUL is going to
happen.*

*SALA smiles and that's precisely it.
It's HORRIBLE, like a wound. A
surge of putrescent adrenalin
creases KEMP. He needs to tell SALA
he doesn't like the smile, but something about it has wiped out his
ability to criticise. What can be
done if everything is SLOW MOTION?
Muscles can't work at this depth.
The swine SMILES again, flopping out
a TONGUE.*

*It protrudes but an inch, waggling
from side to side in imitation of
THE VIPER. Is this an hallucination?
It cannot be, it's HAPPENING.
Suddenly the most god-awful rasp
emits from the bass, like a fucked
hinge on the back gate of hell.*

KEMP

Jesus . . .
          (horrified)
. . . your tongue is like an
accusatory giblet . . .

*The tongue moves a yard from SALA's
face with the accompanying toll of a
drum. It is an anatomical insanity,
an abrogation of all rules pertaining
to the tongue. KEMP is paralysed with
alarm and poleaxed with revulsion.*

*As the TONGUE approaches he pushes
back in his chair like a man on a
crashing plane. Goya drew faces like
this at the moment of death.*

*Here it comes towards him, probing
forth, ever extending as it
explores. It's out four feet, and
then six, a khaki limb, browned at
the root from three and a half
million cigarettes.*

*At twelve feet it seems to have
reached some fearful zenith. It
quivers accusatively before veering
east. KEMP's responsibility is
clear, and he forces his way out of
slow-motion.*

                    KEMP
        For Christ sake, keep it out.

*Grabbing a newspaper he unwalks
forward in a menacing stoop.*

                    SALA
        What are you talking about?

                    KEMP
        Your tongue belongs to Satan.

                    SALA
        Are you out of your mind?

                    KEMP
        Keep it out. It's rotten to
        the root . . . if it goes
        back in your mouth, it'll
        kill you . . .

*He goes for the TONGUE absorbing
toxic spittle in the paper.*

        . . . we gotta get it into
        the sink . . .

                    SALA
                 (standing)
        Stop it. you're giving me fear
        . . . I've got fear . . .

KEMP

So have I . . . fuck you . . .

SALA

. . . you're *high*, you fool,
drink some rum . . .

Drink some rum? That's the best idea
he's heard since 1956.

85 EXT. CONDADO. SAN JUAN BAY. NIGHT.

KEMP and SALA are revealed on a
pier. Ocean one side, distant cruise
ships the other. The rain turned
into mist.

The initial rush of fear has been
superseded by mutual pleasure.

KEMP

Thought I was losing grip in
there.

Strings of multicoloured lightbulbs
disappear into the mist.

What did we take?

            SALA
I don't know.

            KEMP
We need to get some more.

*Swapping hits on a bottle they walk
into the weather. Here and there are
enclaves of slot-machines. Nobody
about and no interest, but further
on is a machine that attracts KEMP.*

*A huge GRINNING LOBSTER reclines on
its top, a claw pointing to a slot
inviting money. Shove in a quarter
and you get to operate a mechanical
crane. The devise hovers over a
filthy aquarium. Should you be
successful you win a LIVING
LOBSTER.*

*A DEAD LOBSTER floats on the mire
and its hapless companions are just
about visible underneath. KEMP can't
believe what he's looking at. He may
have seen such a machine with teddy
bears and trash candy, but never
with PRIZES THAT ARE ALIVE.*

            KEMP
That explains it, doesn't it?

> SALA
>
> Explains what?

> KEMP
>
> The world . . . And us . . .

SALA doesn't know what he's talk-
ing about. There is a separation
of minds. For KEMP this is a
microcosm of the world, and he
might even say so. Blown away by
the LOBSTER MACHINE he clasps
at its sides, forehead pressed
into the glass, staring at the
LOBSTER who is staring back at
him.

> KEMP (V.O.)
>
> I wonder what it is you might
> think about our different
> worlds?

The LOBSTER looks non committal,
KEMP continues to address it.

> KEMP (V.O.)
>
> . . . he looked at me kinda
> sideways and said, 'Human
> beings are the only creatures
> on earth who claim a god, and
> the only living thing that

behaves like it hasn't got
one' . . .

*The CAMERA and the MUSIC close in
on KEMP. He's already into a
dissolve with a clatter of typewriter at the end of it.*

86   INT. SALA'S APARTMENT. DAY.

*Letters like crooked teeth smack
into the paper. KEMP sits at a
table bashing it out on his ancient
portable. Wreathed in cigar smoke,
he wears a towel over his head like
a boxer.*

                    KEMP (V.O.)
Does the world belong to no
one but you? And when he said
it, I was taken aback. Not
because of who was doing the
talking, but because I finally
understood the connection
between children scavenging
for food, and the shiny
brass-plates on the front
doors of banks . .

                    SALA [O.S.]
Gotta go.

*SALA is in and out of the back-
ground, trying to get dressed and
drink coffee at the same time. KEMP
is exhausted, runs hands through the
sweat in his hair. That was a
night, and now there's a knock at
the door. No idea who's there until
he opens it. Too wasted for
surprise. But surprised he is.*

*CHENAULT stands outside looking
abandoned and lost as a refugee. She
probably hasn't eaten and obviously
hasn't slept. You don't need to ask
the questions to know she's in
crisis.*

                    SALA
    We gotta go.

*Too rushed for the bullshit, he's
out as KEMP brings her in.*

                    KEMP
              (to SALA)
    Gimme a minute.

87 INT. NEWSROOM. THE DAILY STAR. DAY.

*Nobody at their desks, but everybody
crowded around LOTTERMAN's office*

*door. The entire journalistic
contingent is here [sports desk,
news desk, editorial, etc] and now
KEMP and SALA. The mood is mutinous
and sour, probably exacerbated by
shouting Scabs and Cop Sirens in the
street below.*

                    KEMP
What's happening?

                  WOLSLEY
A strike.

*KEMP manages to find a better view.
LOTTERMAN is sweating.*

                  LOTTERMAN
. . . it's a big favour I'm
asking, and I know it is . . .
but I'm not asking it for
myself, I'm asking it for the
paper.

                   MOBURG
Such self-sacrifice.

                  LOTTERMAN
. . . I been breaking my ass
for this paper . . . fight-

ing for it, which means,
fighting for you . . .

*They're not buying it and LOTTERMAN
must lie a little harder.*

OK. I'm pleased to tell you
we now have finance in place
with a bank in Miami.

DONAVON
Who's the bank?

LOTTERMAN
You're gonna have to trust me
on specifics, but it's a written
guarantee. I'm just asking for
one more week, then everyone
gets a hundred dollar bonus.

MOBURG
I don't think so.

LOTTERMAN
You have my word of honour.

MOBURG
I can't pay my rent with your
word of honour. This is the
second week we didn't get
paid.

DONAVON
That's right, Fred.

LOTTERMAN
What d'you want, a crucifixion?
I'm doing the best I can.
(re. briefcase)
I'm on my way to sign the
papers, and the longer you
keep me here, the less signed
they get. C'mon, guys, please,
it's Monday, we pull together
till Friday, we can get
through.

They've got no choice and LOTTERMAN
adds a welcome sweetener.

. . . meantime, provided no
one goes crazy, I'll pick up
the tab at Al's.

This seems to do the trick and
everyone drifts back to work.
LOTTERMAN clears sweat with a
handkerchief and notices
KEMP.

How nice of you to drop in.

KEMP

I was covering the carnival.

LOTTERMAN

That's not what I heard, I
heard you were in the moonlight for Sanderson?

*On hands and knees he snatches
various papers from his safe.*

KEMP

I was what?

LOTTERMAN

Moonlighting for Sanderson?

*Slamming the safe he returns to his
desk. More papers from a drawer and
then a framed photo of his seriously
ugly wife.*

KEMP

Where's Segurra?

LOTTERMAN

Mr Segurra is no longer with us.

KEMP

I got a story for you.

LOTTERMAN is too preoccupied to listen no matter what it is.

> LOTTERMAN
> You may have noticed, I'm somewhat busy.

Stuffing documents into his briefcase he's anxious to leave.

> KEMP
> This is real important, involving Mr Segurra . . .
>> *(proffering them)*
> . . . you should take a look at these photographs . . .

> LOTTERMAN
> Let me tell you just how important it isn't.
> I got twenty-one jobs on the line, and a newspaper going under.

> KEMP
> Print this, and you sell it.

Scant attention from LOTTERMAN, already heading out the door.

It's a planning scam . . .
literally despoilation of a
paradise, meanwhile a thousand
people get swept into the sea
like garbage.

LOTTERMAN

You're weird, Kemp . . . it's
not what it's doing to them,
it's what it does to you . . .

KEMP

It's called journalism.

LOTTERMAN

Make me laugh . . . I ask
you to tidy up the booze,
you couldn't sweep out a
room . . .

*Midway up the News Room and everyone
is looking up to listen.*

. . . why d'you think you're
working here? You are everything that's wrong with a
journalist . . .

KEMP

. . . and you are everything

that's wrong with this insult
of a newspaper.

                    MOBURG
Unanimously agreed.

                    LOTTERMAN
Why don't you shut it,
Moburg?
            (beast livid)
If this paper is floundering,
it's because of people like
you . . . eaten away from the
inside by people like you.
You are a waste of human
sperm.

*He ploughs on towards the
exit. Moburg hollering after
him.*

                    MOBURG
Die a prolonged and relent-
lessly agonising death.

88 EXT. DRIVEWAY. BEACH HOUSE. DUSK.

*Such a sunset going down over the
jungle. The music is poignant,
although I don't know what it is.
KEMP stands outside the house while*

SANDERSON tosses his ex-girlfriend's belongings through the front door. No jewels, but dresses, shoes, hats and a clutch of lingerie. An empty suitcase comes last.

> SANDERSON
> Enjoy her.

> KEMP
> Fuck you, Sanderson.

He gathers the satin and lace. Stuffs it into his sidecar.

89 INT. SALA'S APARTMENT. NIGHT.

Now I know what the music is, sad old blues cranking out of SALA's record player. It's a sad old evening, SALA somewhat done on rum, KEMP fixing a mug of hot tea in the Kitchen.

> SALA
> So what's the prognosis?

> KEMP
> She won't talk about it . . .

A kettle whistles and he pours it, heads towards his bedroom.

. . . but I get the idea she went back, and he kicked her out.

> SALA
> How long's she staying?

> KEMP
> She's going to New York.

90 INT. KEMP'S ROOM. APARTMENT. NIGHT.

Last dregs of light at the window. You can always tell when a room's full of misery and this is one. CHENAULT is exhausted with tears. KEMP puts a cup by the bed and quietly sits.

> KEMP
> I made you some tea.

She smiles but doesn't want it, and more tears seem imminent.

You should try and sleep.

                    CHENAULT
I stole your bed.

                      KEMP
It's OK. I'm gonna write.

                    CHENAULT
                (hardly audible)
I'm so sorry.

                      KEMP
Don't be sorry, you did me
the best favour I ever had.

Tears well and she denies them. The
silence belongs to him.

There is no Dream, Chenault
. . . it's just a piss-puddle
of greed, spreading throughout
the world.

91 INT. SALA'S APARTMENT. NIGHT.

Just about as late as it gets. KEMP
hammers his typewriter.

                    KEMP (V.O.)
. . . I want to make a
promise to you, the reader
. . . and I don't know if I

can fulfil it tomorrow or
even the day after that . . .
but I put the bastards of
this world on notice that I
do not have their best interests at heart . . . I will
try and speak for my reader
. . . that is my promise, and
it will be a voice made of
ink, and rage . . .

92 INT. APARTMENT. DAY.

*Wrapped in a gown with a towel over
his head KEMP arrives in the
kitchen. Sleep has revitalised
CHENAULT. Almost herself again,
she's squeezed oranges and made
coffee. KEMP's pleasure is short-
lived, ending wih the woe in SALA's
expression.*

                    SALA
One for you. One for me.

*He hands KEMP a sizable envelope.
Inside is a heart-sinker.*

                    KEMP
Oh man, I would rather not
start the day with this.

CHENAULT

What is it?

SALA

It's a writ.

KEMP
(reading)
Means we're going to court?

SALA

It means they can arrest us,
should they so desire, any
damned minute they like.
(freaked)
We need to speak to a lawyer.

KEMP

We don't even have a phone?

SALA

There's an old guy I know,
Spanish Advocate, he kind of
owes me one . . . You should
get dressed, we'll get over
there.

KEMP

The water ran out, I'm
covered in soap.

Alright, SALA will do what he can. A moment later he's gone. A vacuum of anxiety is left, focusing on rereading the writ.

> CHENAULT
> What's it for?

> KEMP
> I'm afraid it's Hal . . . he put up bond on this thing for us, now he's pulled it.

CHENAULT has something to say. But takes a while to say it.

> CHENAULT
> You know he's a crook, Paul?

> KEMP
> I know he sails close.

> CHENAULT
> They're working a scam with federal grants . . .
> siphoning money into parasite accounts.

KEMP

How?

CHENAULT

He's got a contract with the
city, and a rat on a lead in
the bank, a man called
Green?
    (he remembers him)
When the new money comes in,
they match it with money they
already creamed off, pay out
of the parasite accounts, and
the new money is up for grabs
. . .

KEMP

And we get the writs.

94 INT. SHOWER/BATHROOM/ BEDROOM.
APARTMENT. DAY.

*KEMP picks up the shower where he
left off. Steam and rushing water.
Shampoo runs off and suddenly
CHENAULT is there. He didn't hear
her arrive, but she's here now and
obviously wants to join him. KEMP
isn't arguing as she undresses, bra
and panties evaporate with the
jeans. She steps into the shower*

and turns into the most seductive
thing a naked girl could be with
soap. Hands all over each other,
hands spread over her back and
breasts as her lips are all over
his mouth.

                    CHENAULT
Come to New York with me . . .

                        KEMP
  I will . . .

Nothing between their kisses but
steam and streaming water, and more
whispers inside the embrace, 'come
to bed with me.' He sure fucking
will, and by cinema magic vertical
becomes horizontal. What started in
a bathroom continues on a bed.
CHENAULT's hair drenches the
pillow, clinging to her still
saturated limbs. Although ravenous
for her, KEMP takes it easy with
kisses, jealous of every delirious
moment. Whatever he wants is already
his. But they both want too much
for much more of this and are
about to get it when a voice starts
yelling from another room. To
pretend it isn't happening isn't

*an option. And anyway the volume is
going up.*

*ADOLPH HITLER was a lot of things
but an aphrodisiac he wasn't.
Howling his ludicrous mouth off, he
addresses a rally at Munich. They're
just about to fuck in here when two
hundred and fifty thousand brain-
dead Prussians begin to cheer.*

                CHENAULT
        What is it?

                KEMP
        Hitler.

*Zeig Heil! Zeig Heil! No lovers on
earth could cope with that. To have
any hope it's got to be dealt with
and KEMP wraps himself in a towel.
He knows where it's coming from
and tears the needle off the
record. But doesn't immediately see
MOBURG. Wearing his Nazi Helmet, he
sprawls where he will, a flagon in
action, and drunk as a fucking
beaver.*

                    MOBURG
     It's over.

                     KEMP
     What is?

                    MOBURG
     They shut us down.

*Although possibly expected KEMP is
stunned by the news. He looks
vacantly towards the bedroom.
Hiding in a towel CHENAULT stares
at him from around the bedroom
door. It's just a moment shared, but
might be a moment changing Kemp's
life.*

94 EXT. TERRACE. AL'S BAR. SAN JUAN.
    DUSK.

*Another night congeals over old San
Juan. The piano plays as usual but
doesn't match the mood. A clutch of
redundant work men, principally
journalists, crowd out the terrace.
Many of the faces are recognisable
even if they don't come with names.
One that does is DONAVON and he
seems to be the impresario of corpo-*

rate grief. Everyone shares his
devastation of betrayal.

> DONAVON
>
> He just stood there and lied
> . . . He don't have the
> mortality of a clapped-out
> cash-register.

> HUBERT
>
> It was to avoid severance.

> WOLSLEY
>
> We all know what it was for,
> Charlie, what are we gonna
> do?

> DONAVON
>
> Nothing, there's nothing we
> can do, except report him to
> the Labour Board, which is
> the same as doing nothing.

> KEMP
>
> I disagree. We've gotta strike
> back, nail this bastard to
> his own front door.

DONAVON
And how, pray, do we do that?

KEMP
By printing the paper.

He pushes through tables, commanding a place of prominence.

We got stuff on Lotterman and
his pals, every happy maggot
with his hand in the till.
Maybe the last ever issue,
but we go out in a blaze of
rage.

HUBERT
It cost twenty-two hundred a
shot . . .

KEMP
We bring in the Scabs . . .

DONAVON
They're picketing over money!
You're through the looking
glass. We don't have the
money for drinks.

> WOLSLEY
Reneged on that as well.

> DONAVON
Forget it, Kemp. This has
been coming down the pike for
months, it ain't worth the
fight.

*That just about sums it up, and
everyone just about agrees.*

You gotta know it's over when
it's over, and this lousy little
Caribbean rag is now a wrapping
for fish heads . . .

> WOLSLEY
Plus, it's a lock-out.

> KEMP
Fuck the locks, we walk in.
So hands up who's with me?

*No takers except MOBURG. But what
about the man at the bar?*

Bob?

SALA
(drained)
You *know* I'm with you.

95 INT. SALA'S APARTMENT. NIGHT.

*Fingers flash a light switch. On/
off, on/off, but no light.*

SALA
We didn't pay the bill.

*While SALA hunts for matches, KEMP
looks for something else. Where the
hell is CHENAULT? He pushes into
the bedroom and even in this gloom
can see she's gone.*

*No suitcase no nothing, but back in
the living room he discovers a note
on his typewriter. SALA lights
a candle and KEMP moves in to
read.*

KEMP
She's gone to New York . . .
(single $ bill)
. . . left me a hundred
dollars . . . I don't believe
that, she didn't have any
money.

— 236 —

SALA

You should use it to go with
her, red-eye for fifty bucks.

KEMP

I'm not going anywhere.
          (patrolling)
By some means or another, I'm
gonna put the paper out,
print the bastard, and then
we're gone.

SALA

Face the reality, Paul . . .
no work, no money, (no girl)
and a warrant out for our
arrest?
          (more rum)
There's no contest, Donavon's
right, it ain't worth the
fight.

KEMP

I am not Donavon, I'm not
like the others . . .

*Long shadows follow as KEMP shifts
his anger around the room.*

. . . and I'm telling you,
next time some greasy moron
starts bullshitting me, I'm
going after him, all the way
up to the President of the
United States . . .
I just wanna win one, once
. . . one sheet, if we could
print one sheet . . .

SALA
You ain't gonna get far on a
hundred dollars.

*I don't know about the silence but
SALA heads for the fridge.*

SALA
We're out of rum . . .

MOBURG
It's as if God in a fit of
disgust has decided to wipe
us all out.

*More silence than anybody knows what
to do with. Somewhere probably
Sala's room, a melancholy COCKEREL
echoes the mood.*

MOBURG (COND)
Yea, the cock crows thrice.

KEMP
(like a light)
What about, El Monstruo? Bet
the hundred on El Monstruo?

96 EXT. PANORAMIC. MOUNTAIN LANDSCAPE.
DAY.

*Big music slams in and the view is
bigger still. Wide over mountains
with a distant motorcycle climbing a
country road.*

97 EXT. STREETS. MOUNTAIN VILLAGE. DAY.

*SALA pilots with KEMP on the back
and this time MOBURG is in the
sidecar. A drive-by reveals them back
in the village where El Monstruo
made his celluloid debut. They
rattle their way up a grimy
street, scrawny horses, hens,
and barks from a three-legged dog.
SALA pulls up outside a village
residence.*

MOBURG
How'd you know it lives in
there?

KEMP
I saw it come out.

SALA
You better let me do this on
my own.

*He dismounts and vanishes into the
house with MOBURG staring after.
KEMP looks nervous and gets off to
light a cigarette.*

MOBURG
If he gets it, we'll take it
to Papa Nebo.

KEMP
Who?

MOBURG
My witch doctor . . . she's
an hermaphrodite.

98   EXT. JIBEROS VILLAGE. NIGHT.

A spooky wind puts itself about the almost deserted village. The moon is in and out of racing cloud and the headlight is just better than a candle. The motorcycle cruises the ruts.

> MOBURG (O.S.)
> She drives a garbage truck by day, by night, she becomes Papa Nebo, the hermaphroditic oracle of the dead . . . when permission is granted by Papa Samedi, the keeper of the cemetery, she'll visit to dig up a corpse . . .

They turn into a street full of homesteads built out of junk.

> . . . certain organs of these disgrounded stiffs are indispensable for use in 'ouangas'.

This is it and they pull up. It's a tin-shack with attitude.

99   INT. WITCH DOCTOR'S HUT. NIGHT.

There's a general odour of carcass,
and what with wind rattling the tin
roof, it's not what you'd call a
salubrious abode. Apple-crates to
sit on and a mummified monkey head
on a pike complete the decor.
MOBURG lights a candle revealing an
alter upon which are the Sword and
SACRED BLADDERS.

                    KEMP
This is horseshit, isn't it?

                    MOBURG
She cured my prick.

A disturbing sight just walked in.
Dressed to represent PAPA NEBO, she
wears a mix of male and female togs.
A full white cotton dress is worn
under a Victorian frock-coat with
satin lapels. She's got a top hat
on her head and a human skull
under her arm. A pickaxe [presumably
for digging them up] is carried with
handle down like a walking stick.
All in all, an imposing
presence.

*Within seconds a fire is alight and
PAINTED BONES come out. The prelim-
inaries are brief, MOBURG acting as
intermediary.*

> MOBURG
> She wants to know what you
> want.

> KEMP
> We want her to empower this
> fowl . . . we want it
> blessed, and anything that
> tries to fight it, dead . . .

> MOBURG
> (translating)
> Bring forth the Fowl.

*The PRIESTESS menaces various bones
around the Bird's head, garbling
nonsense like she's throwing up. All
watch with the bated breath as the
ceremony continues, climaxing with
incitement of fire. White-eyed incan-
tations as she throws powder at the
flames. [It's probably some sort of
gun-powder and each handful brings a
devilish gust of smoke.] The BIRD
stands transfixed as everyone else.*

NEBO begins gurgling, calling on the undead to obey and they apparently do.

MOBURG
She says, no fowl on earth could challenge this cockerel and survive.

SALA
Great.

KEMP
How's she off for curses?

MOBURG
Pretty good.

KEMP
Let's have a curse on Sanderson, and that piece of shit in the bank
(with precision)
Green. Mister Green.

The name is transmuted into a curse and she spits out a toad.

SALA
Jesus.

MOBURG

Curse active.

The TOAD fucks off and the COCKEREL crows. NEBO freaks and a fistful of dust lights up like a stage-effect from Aladdin.

100 INT. SPORTING FACILITY. CONDADO. DAY.

Dean Martin may well be singing again. It's a grubby little shit-house, claustrophobic with smut, like the dregs of Las Vegas. Chandeliers hang over a maze of slot-machines, crap tables and right at the end, the ring where they fight birds. Cigarette smoke and cigarette girls selling more. SALA and KEMP sport their best togs, ties even, in an effort to blend in with the tone of the clientele. You put your bet on and get chips in exchange. Odds on the board are understood by SALA, and KEMP defers as $100 goes down. With El Monstruo in its cage, they push through Cariadors, SALA explaining the wager.

> SALA
> It's an accumulator, winnings
> on the win become the next
> bet, it's got to win three.

*Extracting the Big Bird, SALA
deals with the technicalities. I'm
not getting into the mechanics of
this, there's too many angles to
write down. The first Cockerel
pitched against EL MONSTRUO
takes one look and runs for it.
The Monster chases him around the
ring and a clump of feathers later
it's declared void. Jubilation from
KEMP/SALA. 'One down. Two to go.'*

> KEMP
> (re. watch)
> I've got to call Moburg.

*KEMP hangs on to a payphone,
endless ringing tone increases
anxiety. Did he get the number
wrong? He checks his notebook and
re-dials. Once again the phone rings
into a void.*

*EL MONSTRUO is already into the
second fight, murdering the
contender. KEMP arrives back in a*

dilemma. Excitement because his bird is winning, apprehension over the unanswered call. What's worse, the fight, or grotesque faces watching? SALA is too engrossed to hear and KEMP has to wait to speak.

> KEMP
>
> He isn't there.

> SALA
>
> He has to be?

> KEMP
>
> He isn't there.

And his absence is more important to KEMP than anything happening in the ring. His expression is a mix of expectation and foreboding. The gladiators spill feathers and there's a chance of slow-motion. But whatever the action, it is shadowed by the sound of a ringing phone. Almost imperceptible at first, it escalates as the CAMERA closes on KEMP.

101 EXT. REAR OF DAILY STAR BUILDING.
DUSK.

*A dead-end street at the back of
the News Building. Garbage blows in
vortexes, otherwise it's utterly
deserted. Halfway up is a public
pay-phone, ringing endlessly into
nothing. A series of set-ups get
closer and closer to the phone.
Close enough to read numbers on the
dial when at last a hand picks up.
The empty street has already told
the story, and everything MOBURG
says in untrue. 'Where the hell have
you been?'*

MOBURG
I . . . never heard the
phone . . . How's it going?

KEMP [O.S.]
Winning . . . we're winning
. . . is everyone there?
(no answer)
Is everyone there?

MOBURG
Yeah . . . everyone's here.

KEMP [O.S.]
How about Vans?
    (no answer)
How about Vans, Moburg?

MOBURG
Yeah . . . Vans.

102 INT. PAY-PHONE. SPORTING FACILITY.
    NIGHT.

From here KEMP can see across the
facility. SALA is suddenly visible.
Arms in the air he punches with
clenched fists and when he sees
KEMP he does it again. Elation is
instant, and for a moment the phone
is held out as though it can see.

KEMP
    (into phone)
You hear that? You hear it?
We're on our way . . .

103 EXT. STREET. REAR OF DAILY STAR
    BUILDING. NIGHT.

A taxi pulls up at the end of
the street. SALA (plus champion
chicken) and KEMP get out. Before
the latter has paid the fare it's

apparent something is very wrong.
Apart from a lone street light the
place is glum as a grave. No Scabs,
no Vans, no MOBURG. They walk
towards the building with a sense of
enveloping doom. The News Building
is in darkness, steel-mesh security
gates at its rear closed and pad-
locked.

                    KEMP
What the hell's going on? He
said he had the men?

I don't know who finds it, but
there's NOTICE attached to the
gates. Several lines of
legalese conclude with the
only part of killer relevance to
KEMP. He whispers out the
text.

     . . . 'all claims against
     its former owners, will be
     duly considered by the
     receivers signed on behalf of
     First Maritime Bank, Miami'
     . . . by Sanderson's pal, Mr
     Green.

Enough to make a pig spew. Before
KEMP can indulge utter defeat, a
face emerges from the gloom the
other side of the gates.

> MOBURG
> I'm sorry, Paul . . . I
> didn't know how to say . . .
> > *(gesturing)*
> . . . they took the machines
> out . . . not everything
> . . . just the parts that
> matter . . .
> > *(turning away)*
> I'll let you in.

104 INT. COMPOSITOR/PRINT ROOM. DAILY
STAR. NIGHT.

Cavernous and eerie the THREE MEN
and their COCKEREL become a small
part of the print room. KEMP may
check out the machines, but on the
other hand he may not. A profound
sense of failure attends the echoes,
and somehow voices seem detached.

> MOBURG
> It's probably for the best
> . . . we'd probably never
> have pulled it off . . .

> KEMP
All I wanted was a front page.

Footsteps go where they will,
emergency lamps the only light.

> MOBURG
How much did you win?

> SALA
Just under six grand.

> MOBURG
At least you can pay off the
bond.

> KEMP
Screw the bond, we're out of
here.

> SALA
There's a midnight Pan Am?

> KEMP
I'm not risking the airport.
Figure this island owes us a
boat.
> *(a dead smile)*
You smell it? It's the smell
of bastards, but also the
smell of truth.

>   *(a moment more)*
>   I can smell ink.

105 EXT. DOCK ROAD/HARBOUR. SAN JUAN.
    DAWN.

*The motorcycle-sidecar arrives
on the dock and I don't care
who drives. But KEMP is already
gone. He chooses a boat, a
sleek bitch painted black. It's
a nostalgic interlude, made
worse because suddenly it's
clear SALA isn't coming with
him.*

>   SALA
>   I gotta take the hen back.
>   *(embrace)*
>   Find yourself a trade wind.

*A harsh wind blows, KEMP starts the
boat without problem and points it
towards about two hundred million
stars. SALA and MOBURG watch it
pull away but don't hear MUSIC
going with it.*

>   KEMP [V.O.]
>   . . . sure, he'd lived, and
>   he'd lived the way he wanted

. . . 'to live my life like
I want to,' he said, 'is the
least I can do.' And that had
worked for him. And when it
was over, he knew it was over
and required no explanation
. . . he had spent half a
life blowing his brains out
with booze, and the bullet
was just a period at the end
of no sentence in particular.

Hunter S. Thompson
1937—2005